Social Media Marketing Secrets

The Latest Social Media Strategy For the Future on Instagram, Facebook, Youtube and Twitter, Advertising and Seo, Be an Influencer

Jack Gary

© Copyright 2019 by Jack Gary - All rights reserved.

This Book is provided with the sole purpose of providing relevant information on a specific topic for which every reasonable effort has been made to ensure that it is both accurate and reasonable. Nevertheless, by purchasing this Book you consent to the fact that the author, as well as the publisher, are in no way experts on the topics contained herein, regardless of any claims as such that may be made within. As such, any suggestions or recommendations that are made within are done so purely for entertainment value. It is recommended that you always consult a professional prior to undertaking any of the advice or techniques discussed within.

This is a legally binding declaration that is considered both valid and fair by both the Committee of Publishers Association and the American Bar Association and should be considered as legally binding within the United States.

The reproduction, transmission, and duplication of any of the content found herein, including any specific or extended information will be done as an illegal act regardless of the end form the information ultimately takes. This includes copied versions of the work both physical, digital and audio unless express consent of the Publisher is provided beforehand. Any additional rights reserved.

Furthermore, the information that can be found within the pages described forthwith shall be considered both accurate and truthful when it comes to the recounting of facts. As such, any use, correct or incorrect, of the provided information will render the Publisher free of responsibility as to the actions taken outside of their direct purview. Regardless, there are zero scenarios where the original author or the Publisher can be deemed liable in any fashion for any damages or hardships that may result from any of the information discussed herein.

Additionally, the information in the following pages is intended only for informational purposes and should thus be thought of as universal. As befitting its nature, it is presented without assurance regarding its prolonged validity or interim quality. Trademarks that are mentioned are done without written consent and can in no way be considered an endorsement from the trademark holder.

Table of Contents

Introduction 1

Chapter 1: The Influence of Social Media 3
    Search Engine Visibility.. 3
    The Mouthpiece for Your Company 4
    Can Build up Trust with Your Customers.................... 5
    Provides You with a Competitive Advantage............... 6
    Virtually Connect with Your Customers...................... 6
    The Best Business and Sales Leads 7
    A Good Marketing Channel 8
    Why Is Social Media so Important for
    My Business?... 10

Chapter 2: YouTube, Facebook, Instagram, and
            Twitter—How Each Works and
            Which One Is Right for You 13
    YouTube 14
    Facebook... 18
    Instagram.. 20
    Twitter 22
    Which One Should I Choose to Work With? 24

Chapter 3: Facebook and Your Business 27

Why Is Facebook Important for Your Business?..27

Organic Ways to Grow with Facebook 32

Chapter 4: Facebook Marketing 37

Choose What You Want to Promote............................ 37

Choose the Objective of the Ad.................................... 38

Create the Ad That You Want to Promote.................. 39

Target the Ad.. 40

Set the Budget 41

Measure the Results and Learn How to Optimize Your Ads.. 43

Running an A/B Test.. 44

Using the Idea of Geo-Targeting 44

Organic vs. Paid Marketing on Facebook 46

Chapter 5: Instagram Marketing and Techniques 47

Add Hashtags into Your Strategy 48

Join the Instagram Community.................................... 49

Know How Often to Post to Get Optimal Results 49

Have Your Images Work with Your Brand's Vibe.. 50

Learn the Right Ways to Optimize the Entire Profile 51

Understand That Growing Your Followers
Can Be an Art and a Science 52
Be a Follower (We Promise It's a
Good Thing!) 53
Post a Lot of Engaging Videos and Photos 55
How to Turn My Followers into Customers 56
Other Tips You Can Use to Increase
Your Reach with Instagram 58

Chapter 6: Marketing Your Business with YouTube 62

Why Is YouTube so Important? 62
How Can I Grow with YouTube? 63
How Do I Interact with Other People
on My Channel? 66
All About the Videos 67

Chapter 7: Organic YouTube Marketing 71

How to Optimize Your Video to Get the
Most Searches and Clicks 72
What Types of Videos Should I Create
and Share? 73
How to Promote Your Videos as Well as Your
YouTube Channel 76

Chapter 8: Paid YouTube Marketing 79

Working with TrueView 83
A Few Words About Remarketing Your
YouTube Viewers 86

Chapter 9: Using Twitter to Grow Your Business..... 91

    How Is Twitter Different from the Rest? 92

    Finding Your Untapped Market
Through Twitter Chats.. 93

    Always Plan Ahead.. 94

    Make Sure That Your Tweets Are
Always Conversational 95

    Create a Good Tweeting Strategy
and Schedule 97

    Twitter Video 99

    Set Some Goals and Some Milestones 100

    Paid Advertising on Twitter 103

Conclusion.. 107

Introduction

The following chapters will discuss everything that you need to know in order to find the right social media platform to promote your business and how to make it as successful as possible. Social media has taken over the world. Your customers are already online, looking for their news, their favorite businesses, and more. As a business, it is important to create your own presence online so you can meet your customers where they need you most.

This guidebook is going to take time to look at all of the secrets and tips that you need to know to get started with your own social media marketing campaign. We are going to look at the top social media platforms including Facebook, Twitter, Instagram, and YouTube. Each of these social media platforms is full of benefits, and they can ensure that you meet your customer in the right place at the right time.

Building up a presence online and making sure that you provide useful and valuable content to your customers can be hard. And choosing which social media site and platform to go with may seem almost impossible. This guidebook will delve into each of the social media sites and discuss the best marketing strategies to make each one work. Whether you are looking to work with

Instagram, Facebook, Twitter, or YouTube, or some combination of them, you will be able to use this guidebook to help you get started.

There are many different aspects that you have to consider when it is time to start your own marketing campaign, but you can't forget to include your online presence and your presence on social media. Make sure to check out this guidebook to learn everything that you need to know to get started with your social media marketing plan.

CHAPTER 1:

The Influence of Social Media

As a business, if you are not on a social media account yet, or preferably several of them, then it is time to get started right away. Social media has taken over the world. Your friends are on it, your customers are on it, and your competition is already on it. Social media allows you to reach your customers in a more interactive way than ever before. And any business can benefit from having a profile and meeting with their customers online on a regular basis.

Your business needs to have a social media presence. It is the best way to interact with your customers, to talk to them and build up trust, to beat out your competition, to tell more about your company, and to make yourself more visible on search engines. Let's take some time to look at the big influence of social media online and some of the benefits and reasons why you should have a social media marketing strategy prepared right away.

Search Engine Visibility

Every business wants to be able to increase the amount of user engagement and traffic that they have. But, is it really possible to do all of this if your potential customers aren't even able to find you when they go online? There are a number of ways that you can increase the potential customers to your site, but having a good social media profile can help you dominate those first search result pages in a natural and organic way. And this, in turn, increases the profits that you earn.

When you are thinking about this, you can consider the fact that millennials already spend a ton of time on social platforms, and having your own is going to increase the value of your company more than ever. It can not only help you to generate more business and profits for yourself, but it can also stop some of the brand negativity it takes to reach top positions.

The Mouthpiece for Your Company

Whether you have been in the industry for a long time or you are new to the industry, having a positive word of mouth for your business will help you to gain more customers to keep your business running. Social media marketing can be a great way to help you as a business owner interact with your customers and spread more good word of mouth. You can use it to talk about policies in the company, team activities, new launches, and any other information that is needed for the business.

Social networking online can really help your business because you are given a chance to build up a narration that you can use to capture the interest of your customers.

Each post that you do on Facebook and each tweet on Twitter can share the values and ethics of the company, along with the product, and can go so far in promoting you and your business.

One thing to keep in mind here is that, while social media can be a great mouthpiece for your company, that doesn't mean that you should flood everyone with a ton of posts all the time. Writing a post twenty times a day is going to get excessive and will annoy your customers. Posting a few times is fine, but make sure that everything you post is relevant and will provide some value to your customers.

Can Build up Trust with Your Customers

No matter where you advertise to your customers, whether it is online or not, you will find that you have to build up trust with your customers or they are never going to choose your products over the competition. This is even more important when it comes to social media because you don't get a chance for the customer to come and meet up with you—they have to do it all online.

Social media and the presence that you can build upon there has become so important when it comes to earning the trust of your customer. You can make your business and see it survive without needing a physical store. But, without a good presence on social media, your customers won't know who you are and they may not even give you a chance.

Provides You with a Competitive Advantage

Take a look at some of the things that your competitors are doing. How many of them are finding social media as a good way to reach their own customers. Do you think that your competitors thought it was smart to ignore social media and stay off of it? You are going to be wrong on this one. There is a big chance that your competitors are already investing both their money and their time on at least a few social media sites in the hope of making a positive presence and gaining business. If you aren't doing this and you aren't willing to learn how to do this, then you are going to be at a big disadvantage.

You will find that not giving your business a good presence on social media means that you are missing out on all of the good benefits that come from these platforms. And when you pass on the benefits, this automatically benefits your competition more. So, it may be a good idea to check into social media and see what it can do for you.

Virtually Connect with Your Customers

When you aren't able to meet with your customer face to face, it is sometimes hard to convince them that your product is the best one for them to go with. It is critical that as a virtual company, one who sells their items online and tries to market and sell products online, that you can prove your credibility and gain the confidence and trust from your customers.

You will quickly find that these social media platforms are going to give you the opportunity to create a good bond with your customers. Your brand has to know that it is so important to engage with your customers, and using social media can be one of the best ways to help promote your services. You can showcase the products you have, give testimonies, and even interact with customers so that they have a chance to engage with your business any time that they want.

The Best Business and Sales Leads

One of the main reasons that a lot of companies choose to go on social media is to help them generate leads, and social media can do wonders for making this happen. And with the help of some social media channels like YouTube and Pinterest, which allow direct purchases, the game of social media is even more powerful than before. Instagram has even jumped on board with this new trend and launched their own call to action button, one that is going to help its audience to shop and install any application that it needs.

This makes it easier for your business to reach your customers. With interactive posts and lots of pictures to showcase your products and services, you can really reach customers and even make the sale. The added bonus comes when you can have a little 'Buy Now' button on your post so customers don't have to search around in order to purchase any item they want, making things easier than ever.

The world of social media is evolving and changing very fast, and it is going to help you drive sales in a big way. If you don't make this a part of your marketing strategy and work to sell your products there, then it is going to be very hard for you to beat out the competition.

A Good Marketing Channel

As a business, you want to make sure that you can drive sales well. This is one of the biggest merits that come from using a social network site. All of the various channels of social media that you will use have their own marketing machinery in place. Each of them works in slightly different ways, but these marketing options are going to make it easier for your brand to connect with the audience that you are targeting. For example, the Sponsored Posts from Facebook and Twitter's Marketing Campaign are two of the most popular ways to market your products and services.

One of the nice things that you will find with a variety of social media channels is that they have their own unique marketing options. They have developed their marketing options in order to improve the reach that you can make with your audience. Though you don't always need to have a good presence in social media to use these channels, but it can help. Many global brands link a lot of their marketing campaigns with the social profiles that they create to increase both likes and followers.

If your business hasn't been able to get into social media yet, the time is now. The power that comes with social media is huge, and you will be amazed at the number of doors that it can open up to bring more success to your business, as long as you use it in the right manner. Benefits that are generated by various social media channels are measurable and so many companies have the results behind them, therefore, there really isn't a reason that you shouldn't take advantage of it as well.

There are a lot of benefits of using social media and getting the most out of using it. There are a ton of different sites out there that you can choose from, and you are sure to enjoy the different options as they help you reach your overall goals. You have to be careful about choosing the right social channels and make sure that you have a detailed strategy in order to make this all work.

Just posting some images on occasion and doing status updates is not going to be enough to help you run your business. Finding the right combination of informative and promotion posts and targeting your posts to meet with your audience are required in order to generate the desired results. In addition, being able to generate the leads that your business needs from advertising on social media can be a new ballgame which can really help your business to grow.

Why Is Social Media so Important for My Business?

We are going to spend some time in this guidebook talking about social media and the different ways you can use it to help promote your business. But why should you consider using social media? Isn't the marketing plan that you already have working well, and isn't it enough to help you grow your business?

There are many other ways that you can market your business and still reach your potential customers. You can work with radio and television advertisements. You can work with an email campaign. You can send out fliers, work with putting ads up online, and so much more. And all of these should be considered when you are working on your own marketing plan.

But, if you choose to ignore the power of social media, you are really leaving something important on the table. Social media can get you in touch with your customers, right where they are. Most of the advertising that you will do on social media is very affordable, especially when you compare what you get out of it; it is very cost efficient. When you want to make sure that your budget can last as long as possible, then working with Facebook, Instagram, YouTube, and Twitter can be one of the best ways to do it.

Another benefit is that you are going to see some great results when you try to personalize yourself with the customer. There are a lot of different companies out there for your customers to choose from. If they don't see your personality and what sets you apart from others, then they won't really have a reason to choose you over someone else. Using social media to open up and really showcase your business can be a fantastic way to seem more personal with your customers, and it can help you get more profits in the long run.

Your customers are already on social media; they are there in large numbers and ready to spend their money. This alone should be enough reason to get you to consider advertising your business through social media. If you pick out the right platform and learn how to use it in the most optimal and efficient manner, you can reach your customers right where they are, and this alone can do wonders for helping you see amazing results with the growth of your business.

And finally, if you don't take advantage of social media, then your competition will. Do you really want to give your competition a leg up on you simply because you refuse to be on social media, and at least use it a bit in your marketing plan? Your competition is already working closely with one or more social media sites, interacting with their customers and trying to gain more business. If you want to get a piece of the pie, then you need to do the same.

Social media, whether you use Facebook, Twitter, YouTube, or Instagram, can be a great way to grow your business, to make sure that your reputation is doing well, and so much more. You will be able to pick out which one will work the best for you based on the type of customer you work with, the product that you sell, and more. Make sure to check out the other chapters in this guidebook to help you learn more about each social media site and how you can use each one to help promote your business.

CHAPTER 2:

YouTube, Facebook, Instagram, and Twitter—How Each Works and Which One Is Right for You

There are a lot of social media platforms out there. Some platforms cater to a certain demographic, and others are there to reach the customer as a whole. There are too many of these platforms to spend time on, so in this chapter, and the rest of the book, we are going to focus mainly on looking at the four big names, YouTube, Facebook, Instagram, and Twitter, to get an idea of how they work and who will benefit from each one the most.

One note here is that while all of these social media platforms have a huge reach and lots of potential customers, not all of them may be right for you. Depending on the business you are in and where your customers are at, you may have to limit yourself to just using one or two. You also have to be careful about not spreading yourself out too thin. It is easy to agree to work on ten social media sites and then feel overwhelmed by the work that needs to be done. If you only choose one or two social media sites to work on, you will find it is much more effective compared to not being able to keep up with a bunch of them.

Let's take a look at the top four social media platforms for your business and get a good idea of which one is the right one for you.

YouTube

YouTube is the first platform that we are going to take a look at. This one is often not seen as a social media platform because it doesn't meet some of the traditional outlines that the others do. But making videos and posts for your customers on this platform will help you to grow your business. Creating videos takes some more time compared to just writing out a quick post, but it can really make a difference in the reach that you can get to your customers.

The first question here is why you should consider marketing on YouTube. There are a lot of benefits that come with marketing on YouTube that many businesses don't consider fully. The first is that video is a huge thing right now. It is actually taking over the world of marketing, and if you aren't using a video, you are going to find that the competition is already ahead of you. And this isn't a joke. Video ranks higher on all of the social platforms out there, which means that customers are more likely to notice and respond to businesses that use a video compared to those that just do a regular post.

When you decide to use the YouTube platform, you are going to have a big library of videos that you can use. You can choose to go through and upload your video files natively to every platform. Or, there is the option to embed the videos into your blog posts, just with a few clicks, which can help you to make the blog posts more engaging and dynamic.

Another benefit is that YouTube already has a very big and diverse audience and many of the people in that audience are going to work with both the search engine on Google and YouTube to help them find any content that they want. If you are good at optimizing your keywords to go along with the videos, you will be able to have an instant connection with your audience, rather than hoping that the right ads on Facebook will show up on the newsfeeds for your customers.

Any business who decides to work with YouTube will find that they have a large potential audience group that they can work with. You just have to find ways to make high-quality videos and use the right keywords so you can reach those customers and get them to make a purchase. Add in that these videos from YouTube can also show up near the top of search results for Google, this can make it easier for your customers to find the videos that you are posting.

And the final benefit is that there are not that many businesses that are using YouTube right now. While you can go online and find so many videos, only about 9% of small businesses are using YouTube. This means that you will gain an edge over the competition because there isn't as much found on this platform. If you can create high-quality and entertaining videos, you could easily get in early and beat out the competition, resulting in more sales along the way.

To really see some success when you get started with YouTube, you must ensure that your approach is different than what you see on other social media platforms. The other options that we will talk about will revolve around the idea of creating and sharing great content with the goal of creating conversation, engagement, and awareness. This is basically all about socializing online.

But with YouTube, things are a bit different. These videos that you will post are more similar to blog posts than anything else, and they are going to fit in more effectively to content marketing. Yes, there are times when people will comment, but these comments are going to be similar to the way they comment on a blog post, not an active discussion like we see on other posts. Your customers are going to come to your profile to view and digest videos, rather than share their thoughts about the day. This is why any marketing that you do on YouTube should be seen more as content marketing rather than social media marketing.

Some of the key points that you should remember when working with marketing your business on YouTube include:

1. People who find your videos on YouTube are going to find them when doing a search or when they view other content that is related. On most social media sites, outside of Pinterest, they may see you if they follow you, if they see your information from ads, or if one of their friends engaged with you.

2. The emphasis that comes with YouTube is to watch videos, not spend time discussing them. You don't really see a lot of people tagging others when they do comment like they might in other sites. Remember that YouTube is more about the experience of the viewer, rather than a social one. If someone wants to, they will decide to share it on the platform of their choice.

3. Many people are going to come to YouTube because their intention is to sit down and watch a video. They probably won't get there and idly scroll through the feed like they might with Facebook.

When you learn how to approach your YouTube channel as a platform with good content, rather than a social one, you will find that it is easier to create stronger videos, ones that your potential customers will like and ones that can perform well.

Facebook

The next social media platform that you may want to take a look at is Facebook. Facebook has been the leader in social media for many years now, and it is often the first place that businesses are going to look when it is time to promote their businesses. They know that there are a ton of customers on the page, and if they use insightful and useful posts along the way, they will be able to reach their target audience.

Facebook is still one of the largest social media platforms out there, and this is naturally one of the first places that a lot of companies choose to go with. You will be able to reach a lot of customers, and Facebook has a variety of options available to you to help reach your customers. You can choose to set up a business page where you can interact with your customers, share information, and discuss things with them.

You have the option of doing a classic ad, do a promotion, promote one of the posts that you put on one of your pages, do a sponsored page or past, work with an open graph to help you label the actions of your users and learn more about them, and so much more. No social media site has as many options as Facebook, which is part of why it is such a great social media platform for you to choose to work with.

There are also a lot of advertising features that you can use when you decide to use Facebook as your main social media platform. Some of the features that you will be able to see when you use Facebook advertising include:

- Built-in ad performance measurement tools
- Ad testing, which means that you can send out several versions of an ad at the same time for you to compare which one works the best before deciding
- The ability to set up the budget you want to work with when you send out an ad
- Help with demographic targeting based on interests, education, location, and age

What this means is that Facebook has a lot of the tools and features that you can look for in order to improve your business and to target your customers. You can measure how an ad is doing, check and see which version out of several ads seems to have the best response, and so much more.

Not everyone is going to see some benefits when they go with Facebook. While there are a lot of benefits and Facebook can provide you with the audience and the tools that you need to really see your business grow, you will find that, sometimes, it isn't right. Don't just go right into marketing on Facebook just because it is the biggest name out there, unless you know for sure that you will be able to reach your audience. Depending on the type of business you are and the products you sell, it may be more efficient to work with a different platform.

This isn't to turn you from Facebook. Many companies will still choose to go with Facebook because of all it has to offer. But Facebook doesn't have every audience out there, and it can get expensive, especially if you aren't even reaching the right customers. Doing your research ahead of time ensures that you are reaching your customers and choosing Facebook because it is the right option, not just because everyone else is doing it.

Instagram

The next option that you can choose to work with when it is time to promote your business is Instagram. Instagram is quickly growing in popularity, and with all of the great features, such as a 'Buy Now' button that you can add into your posts, it is easy to see why so many people want to move into advertising and marketing through Instagram.

Instagram is a picture-sharing site. It works similarly to other social media sites, but for this one, you are going to focus your energy on providing high-quality pictures first, and then good descriptions second. The first thing people are going to notice when they come to your Instagram profile is the pictures that you have.

Everything is about pictures, and if you put ones up that don't relate to your business or you pick out ones that aren't high-quality, then customers are going to turn away, and you will never see results.

It has become clear recently that Instagram isn't just a site for personal use. It is a global platform that makes it easier for companies and various brands that humanize their content, showcases all of their products, recruit the new talent that they need, and even to inspire their audience. And all of these can be done with the right pictures that show up on your page.

The nice thing that happens with the users of Instagram is that they just aren't active, but they also engage with you. This video and picture sharing app is now becoming one of the top sites for social media. In fact, over half of the active users on the site are on it each day, and 35% of those say that they check the account for more than one time a day.

What this means is that there is a huge amount of potential for your business to grow through this platform. Instagram is a good way to introduce some of your products and can make it easier to grow more brand awareness. In fact, research has shown that at least 70% of users on Instagram have spent some time looking up a brand on that specific social media platform.

Instagram allows you to promote your brand and your product in a way that is authentic and friendly, without having to focus on using hard selling tactics that never work and can turn your customers off from the product. If you can provide high-quality products to your customers and can even share some good videos, you will find that Instagram may be the social media site that works the best for you.

You will find that many businesses are starting to move over to Instagram as a way to promote their business. But, it is still relatively new and there is a lot of room for your business to grow. We will discuss some of the different ways that you can really promote yourself on this social site, but providing high-quality pictures, interacting with your customers, and playing around with different hashtags and timings for the posts can make a difference in the results that you can get with this platform.

Twitter

And finally, we need to take a look at Twitter and what it can do for your business. Twitter currently has more than 313 million monthly active users, and most of the demographic are younger, which makes it perfect for most marketers and businesses. Getting started on Twitter is pretty easy as well because anyone can pick out the right Twitter handle, upload a profile picture, fill out the bio, and then send out a tweet or two. The issue that comes up is learning how to grow the account and how to turn it into a tool that will build your brand and bring in leads.

You will quickly find that growing the type of customer base that you want with Twitter is going to take a bit more than sending out tweets only when the company has a big event or when a new product is being released. It is more about engaging with your target audience and then finding ways to interact with them in meaningful and valuable ways.

The first question that you may have when it comes to Twitter is: how this social media site is different from the other options that we have talked about so far? Understanding the way that Twitter works, especially when compared to other social media sites, can ensure that you get the most out of your Twitter marketing plan.

There are actually a lot of different ways that businesses use Twitter to help with their marketing and some of these include:

- Managing their reputation
- Branding
- Networking
- Letting them interact with their customers
- Driving engagement for promotional activities
- Sharing information and content

Most of these have something to do with your interactions and how you get along with the customers you have. It is not all about broadcasting your content, like what you will see with Pinterest. Twitter is more about communication and keeping those lines open with your customer.

If you are looking for a different way to meet with your customers and to have more communication and interaction with them compared to some of the other sites, then Twitter is the right option for you. Twitter has so many different options that you can choose to go with to help you market, and it has changed so much in the past few years to include more services and more neat things to help you grow your business.

Twitter is a bit different compared to some of the other platforms. It is more about opening up a conversation with your customer, something that can be done with the other options, but isn't always done. If you can open up the lines of communication with your customer and you are ready to have a conversation with your customers, you will find that Twitter is the best social media platform for you.

Which One Should I Choose to Work With?

As you can see, all of the social media platforms that we have talked about can be a great way to promote your business. They provide so many options to choose from and so many ways that you can interact with your customers. But spreading yourself out to so many different areas can be hard to do. Most marketing plans need to have a solid focus on just one or two social media platforms to ensure they can reach their customers in the right place, without wasting time, effort, and money. So, how do you choose the right one for you?

The answer really depends on the kind of business you run and how you think you can really beat out your competition. Going where the customers actually are and meeting them in a new and innovative way, rather than just following the competition or picking one because it sounds neat, is the best way to make sure that you pick out the right social media site.

If you know that most of your target audience is on Facebook, and you think you can interact and get in contact with them the easiest that way, then this is the method that you should use. But if you find that videos may be the best way to showcase your products or could be a better way to reach your customers that the competition hasn't gotten to yet, then YouTube may be a good option.

For those companies that know a picture is worth a thousand words and who have a ton of great products that would look amazing in pictures, then Instagram may be a good option. Or, if you want to really open up communication with your customers and want to work on building up your reputation online, then Twitter may be the way to go.

When you are first getting started with your social media marketing campaign, make sure that you pick just one or two to start with. This allows you to get really familiar with the audience on there and the way the platform works. You can always add in more sites later on and even drop some if you want, but starting out with a few can be the best use of your budget money and ensures you really get a chance to use them properly before adding in more.

CHAPTER 3:

Facebook and Your Business

Facebook is one of the biggest social media platforms out there. Everyone has heard of Facebook, and many people have a personal profile to help them connect with others, look at the news, and even follow some of their favorite companies. While you may use Facebook with a business page and in a different manner than your customer, it is still a great way for you to connect with customers and lead to sales.

Let's take a closer look at Facebook and some of the reasons that your business needs to consider setting up a presence organically on this social media site.

Why Is Facebook Important for Your Business?

Facebook is one of the largest social media sites out there. Almost everyone you talk to is going to agree that they have a Facebook account and that they use it on a regular basis, most people are on at least one time each day. This means that there is a huge pool of current and potential customers on this site that you can reach, resulting in most sales than ever. While it is going to take some creativity to find ways to reach out to your customers in a new and innovative way that others haven't already done, there is still a lot of great reasons to choose to go with Facebook for your business.

There are a lot of different parts of Facebook, and businesses that can learn about and understand how this system works the best are the ones that get ahead. Some of the things that you need to know about Facebook and why it is so important to use it in your own marketing campaigns and plans includes:

1. *There are more than 400 million users around the world*: Facebook has recently announced that it passed the mark for 400 million members. This means that if Facebook were a country, it would be the third largest in the world. Think of all the potential customers you can reach here.

2. *100 million users from the U.S.*: Out of the numbers that we listed above, 100 million of those users come from the United States. This is a huge target audience for you to use, even here in the United States.

3. *The average user spends 55 minutes on this site each day*: This is almost an hour a day. This is a lot of time to spend on Facebook, which gives you plenty of opportunities to reach out to your customer and get them to look into your products.

4. *80,000 sites are working with Facebook Connect*: Connect is an initiative through Facebook that has the greatest long-range impact. By integrating with Facebook closely, sites are making social graphs easier to use and more portable. Instead of heading to Facebook and other sites to visit with friends, the participants can travel with Facebook and see what is going on at all times. Even sites like Myspace and Yahoo! are starting to come in with these integrations.

5. *The average user on Facebook has 130 friends*: This means that you have a lot of room to grow your business. If you can get just one person interested in your products, they may be willing to share their love of the product with their friends. This is an extra 130 impressions that you can earn.

6. *The average user on Facebook will become a fan of four pages each month*: If you think that your customers are quickly going to become big fans of the Facebook page that you set up for the company without doing much work, then you have to pull back a bit on your expectations for the work. The average user is only going to become a fan of four pages each month. This isn't a ton considering how many different organizations, causes, and brands we are in contact with on a regular basis.

7. *The wall posts you have won't impact popularity*: A study that was done by Sysomos found that there isn't really much correlation between how often you post on the wall and how many fans there are. However, there is a strong connection between the amount of other content, such as videos, photos, links, and notes, and how many fans you have. If you want to work with Facebook and you are looking to increase your fan base so you can reach more people, it is important that you move yourself beyond the simple wall posts. Adding in things like links, videos, and photos, to name a few, can help you out.

8. *Facebook has a customized News Feed*: Facebook recently made a move to an algorithm-driven news feed. What this means is that just because someone has become your fan, it doesn't mean they are going to always see your status updates or wall posts. This is true when we look at business and individual posts. Instead, the news feed is going to be set on default based on the content Facebook things you will lack. This is all based on interactions with content from the author in the past and interactions by your friends on that content.

This can put a lot of premium on posting content that is more engaging and will be more likely to get the shares, comments, and likes that you want. If you are not already paying attention to the analytics you get from Facebook, then now is the time to do so. You can look at your engagement scores and then mess around with some different types of content to see what would work the best for you.

There are many reasons why you should choose to work with Facebook as part of your marketing campaign. It is one of the largest platforms for social media right now, meaning that you get the benefit of reaching a ton of potential customers in an organic way. You also have a ton of options when it comes to advertising with Facebook, with many tools that Facebook has set up specifically to handle all of your business needs.

Now, if you are looking to get your business up and running on Facebook, you must first set up your own business page. This is relatively simple to do. Facebook will ask you a few questions, and then you can go in and fill out the rest of the parts and the rest of the sections. Make sure you provide a link to your website, add in some pictures, and fill in the About Me section. If you have a physical location as well, it is a good idea to add this into the page. The more complete the page is, the better things will be, whether you use organic or paid reach to get customers there.

It is also a good idea to spend your time writing out a few posts. No customer wants to come to your business page and see nothing there. Even as a beginner, get into the habit of posting on a regular basis. There might not be a ton of customers in the beginning, but it won't take long before more show up, and they will have a much better time interacting with you if they see there is already a lot of content there.

Organic Ways to Grow with Facebook

When it comes to advertising on Facebook or on any other site that you choose to use, you have two options: you can choose to grow your reach organically or with paid advertising. Growing your reach organically can be a nice method to use because you are surer that the customers who come to you really want your products or your information. And most organic methods are cheap or free so it helps your budget. However, these methods are much slower than what you can get with an advertisement, and you will find that it can take several months to several years to get the same reach organically as you can with paid advertising, especially when you are on Facebook.

With that said, it is best if you can do some combination of the two options. Organic reach can still be done, even if you are still using paid advertising to get the customers to you. In fact, this can help you get the most results for the least amount of money overall. Let's take a look at some of the steps you can take in order to organically grow your own business with the help of Facebook.

There are many things that you can do in order to grow the organic reach that you want when you are on Facebook. Keep in mind that this organic reach is often going to be at a slower pace than you may want, but it can build up some really great customers, the ones who are actually interested in your product, who may already be searching for your product, and who may be more willing to share the posts that you have. Some of the best things that you can do to increase your organic reach on Facebook include:

- *Build up your authority and your presence*: Your customers are going to come to you because they think you are the expert or the authority on a topic. Taking the time to show this in your posts and the items that you put on your business page can go a long way in bringing in more customers and keeping them around.

- *Make sure that your content is evergreen*: An evergreen content is a content that isn't going to be out-of-date in a few weeks, months, or even years. This is a content that can provide value to your customers and will serve them well whether they look at the information right then or they look at it a few weeks down the road. Sure, it is fine to have a limited time promotion for your business on occasion, but the majority of the content that you place on your profile or your business page should be evergreen for your customers.

- *Post when the competition is sleeping*: There can be a lot of noise on Facebook if you are not careful. Instead of going through and posting when all of your competition does and risk being drowned out by it all if you can do so and you notice that your customers are still responding well, try to post at times when the competition is pretty quiet. This ensures that you get to be front and center, without any other noise in the process.

- *Test how often you should post for the best results*: There is a lot of advice out there on how many times you should post, and even when you should put your posts up on a Facebook business page. But the trick here is to find the time that seems to work the best for your customers, and then do your posting there. This will help you to reach your customers where they are, whether it is in the morning, afternoon, or night. Some companies may find that they need to post more often, while some may only need to post once or twice a day. Look through your Facebook analytics and determine the right times for you to do your posting.

- *Let your email list do some of the work*: If your business has been growing for some time, then you may already have a good email list that you could try out. This email list can be used for a variety of things, but one option is to promote your Facebook page a little bit. This doesn't have to be done all the time, but letting your email list customers know that you have this page and that they can get exciting updates on there, can be a good way to get more people to follow you on Facebook.

- *Run a contest*: Nothing is better to organically grow your customer base than running a contest. You can choose the method you want to use to run this contest, but make sure that the incentive is one that will get other people to pay attention to what you are offering. You can use this to get more sales, to get more followers, or for a combination of the two.

- *Use copy that is persuasive and will grab attention*: The copy that you write on your business page is going to be so important when it comes to how much attention you will get from your customers. You want a copy that is friendly, persuasive, and will grab the attention of your customers. When it comes to advertising on Facebook, remember that your customers may see hundreds of posts a day. You must find some way to stand out from the crowd.

- *If you are going to use hashtags, use them in the proper manner*: Hashtags can be used on Facebook, even though they are most commonly used with Twitter. But you shouldn't just use a hashtag just because the option is there. You need to be strategic about the way that you use these hashtags. Pick out ones that are unique, ones that go with your business name or ones that your customers are more likely to look for when they want to find your business.

- *Make sure that you focus more on providing value than on your reach*: Sometimes, we get so caught up in trying to get more reach, and our content is going to suffer. Poor content on the business page is not going to keep your current customers around, and it definitely won't bring in any new potential customers either. Make sure that you focus your attention on providing value to your customers, and the rest will take care of itself.

No matter what plan you choose to go with for your Facebook marketing campaign, make sure that you include at least a few of these tips for growing the page organically. Even when it comes to some of the paid advertising that you want to do, things like evergreen content, and providing some kind of value to your customers can not only help increase your organic reach but can also make your advertising more effective.

CHAPTER 4:

Facebook Marketing

While you will want to take some time to work through some of the steps to organically grow your content, like what we talked about previously, many companies have started to look towards Facebook advertising in order to help them. Finding all of the customers that you need can be hard, especially when you consider how much competition and noise is already on the social media site. Working with paid advertising can actually make a big difference because it allows you to get your ads right in front of your target audience when you need it the most.

Facebook makes it easy for you to create your very own ads. You can choose to release just one ad, do an A/B testing to see how each one works, and then pick and more. Facebook even makes it easy for you to pick out a whole campaign so you can get the most out of your work and budget. Let's take a look at some of the steps that you can take to create your own ad for Facebook and how to get the most out of your budget when you decide to do paid advertising.

Choose What You Want to Promote

This is going to be different for everyone involved. Some people want to be able to promote their business and just increase brand awareness. Some people want to increase their reach and will advertise in this manner. And, still, others may choose that they want to sell a new product or a campaign of products and increase their sales.

You can choose any of these categories that you want and more, but you have to come up with a clear idea of what it is before you even start. Each of these categories will require different things to occur, and they will each shape what is going on with your campaign and the decisions that you make. Facebook helps with this because it will provide you with the opportunity to promote your Facebook place or page or an external URL, such as your website. You just have to choose which one you want.

Choose the Objective of the Ad

Now, it is time to get down to the nitty-gritty and determine what the objective of the ad should be. Are you looking to see if you can increase the number of likes that you can get on the page? Are you looking to promote a particular post in order to get more views and maybe more purchases?

Many businesses are going to work to promote a post. This allows them to get some more likes on a page and more eyes paying attention to them. And in many cases, the post is set up to help advertise the business or a particular product that they are trying to sell to their customers.

Another thing that you can try out is to promote a post that can link back to a particular blog article for your business (if you don't already have a blog up and running, it is time to get it done), and this would then lead the customer to a landing page to help with lead generation.

Create the Ad That You Want to Promote

From here, we need to go through and actually create the ad that our potential customers are going to see on their news feed. If you have never gone through and done this process in the past, it can seem a bit daunting. But Facebook has things set up to make it easier for you; you simply need to follow the right steps, and you will be fine.

First, let's look at what you need to do if you plan on using this advertisement to promote your own page. To do this you need to work with the following:

- Upload an image that is at least 100 px by 72 px. This is often going to be your logo, but you can also choose another image that fits your needs or the needs of the advertisement. Make sure that it is high-quality and will actually help promote your business.

- Create a headline. If you are just trying to promote your own page, then Facebook will go through and do this for you. When Facebook puts this information in, it is going to be the company name that was added into your file.

- Now, you need to create the ad text. You are given 90 characters to write out a small description of your business. You can either write out your own and make it persuasive and catchy or the default is the description for your business that you wrote on your page.

If you want to promote a post instead, the ad that you are doing will simply hold the post of your choice. It is as simple as that!

Target the Ad

One of the most important decisions that you will make when it comes to your ad and your promotion is how to target it. It is a huge waste of money if you just send out the ad with a bunch of guesses because you are likely to send it to the wrong demographics. Basically, you need to know your audience, what they like to do, and where to reach them.

If you don't already know your target audience, then it is time to get to work. You are going to just waste your time and money if you don't have this information, so get together with your marketing team and figure it out.

Once that is done, you will be better prepared to target your ad to the right people.

Facebook will provide you with four ways to segment out your audience. These will include:

- Target by the geographic location: You get the choice to target your ad based on the country, state, city, zip code, and more of your customer.

- You can target by the age or the gender.

- It is possible to go through and target by interest. This is where you are able to segment out your advertising in order to pinpoint the audience that you would like to reach. For example, if you are running a specialty running store, you would choose some interests like exercise, fitness, marathons, and running. Then, you would make sure that with this segmentation that your add is only going to show up to those who have already shown themselves interested in the topics that you chose.

- Target by the connection status. For this one, you will choose to show your ad to the individuals who are already connected to your page.

Set the Budget

Facebook also allows you to be in full control over the budget that you work with. You can set a daily budget that you want to stick with for each day of the campaign or a total campaign budget for Facebook to work with. If you are just starting out with this, it is a good idea to do a smaller budget, and then as you optimize the strategy that you are using with advertising, you can spend more on the budget.

One thing to note with the budget on Facebook is that it is set so that the ad is going to run continuously. Make sure that you go through and add a start date and an end date to this ad. This helps you to be more in control over how long the advertisement is going to run with. As a beginner, you may find that a smaller campaign that runs for 7 days and has a budget of $10 a day is a good place to start.

When you are setting the budget up, you can choose to be charged with a cost per impression or a cost per click depending on your overall goals. If you are trying to promote your page and you want to get the maximum amount of page likes possible, the default charge is going to be charged each time that someone sees the ad within the defined target audience, which means you are being charged a cost per impression. If you are trying to promote a post that will link back to your website, then the default is to charge you cost per click, which means that you will only be charged when someone actually clicks on your ad and is redirected to your posts.

Also, Facebook may have times when it goes slightly over your budget if it thinks that it can really use the money to promote better on one day or another. This means that the daily budget will be taken a bit over, but your campaign budget will still end up the same; one of the other days will just get a bit less money. So, if you are doing a campaign that is $10 a day for 7 days, you will still spend only $70 on the campaign, but you may spend $15 on a day and $7 on a couple other days to cover it.

Measure the Results and Learn How to Optimize Your Ads

It is never a good idea to place an ad or promotion on Facebook and just ignore it. Many people forget that they should use some of the analytic tools that are available through Facebook to help them make smart decisions about their business and to help them to optimize their ads so they get the most out of the process.

You can use Facebook analytics to help you do this. This analytics help you to see how much you spent, which days you spent the most, how your customer seemed to react to the work that you were doing, and more. There are a lot of insights that you can get when it comes to working with this analytics, and you are really just harming your own business if you aren't willing to look at them. These insights can give you a lot of information on how to improve and make your future ads so much better.

Running an A/B Test

One option that you may want to consider when it comes to your Facebook page is running A/B testing. What this includes is taking two ads that are pretty similar, but with little differences in them. You may use this when you have two ads that may be really good, and you want to see which one would do the best. You would work on both of the ads, and then send them out at the same time to see how customers respond.

The budget for each ad has to be the same, and they are usually pretty small because you are doing a small test run. You can then watch the analytics on each one and determine which one is sticking around and which is going to be your main campaign. This is a great way to reserve your budget while also reducing your risk because you know exactly which advertisement your customers will respond to the best.

Using the Idea of Geo-Targeting

This is a way to pin a certain audience for a specific geographic. This is one of the most direct ways to direct your message and a very effective and powerful to boost your efficacy. With just a few clicks on Facebook, you have a new ad that's ready for advertising. But, of course, there's a catch—there is no easy route when conducting business. Taking this route can really jack up the price of your campaign.

Attracting higher value customers, businesses can benefit from this method whether it's a real estate company looking for a higher source or a B2B business looking to amplify a higher average to attract new business that will pay more for the growth of the company.

Your business can use this method to help them find some new customers. You can place your physical location and then make advertisements to local customers. With regular outbound sales, this process could cost you thousands of dollars. But Facebook Ads can do the work for you without all the hassle.

In order to target the group that you want, you can just set up an ad with Facebook as usual. When you get to the audience, you can drop a pin in the area where you are located. This shows the program where you are located and that you want to reach other customers in the same area. After you have dropped the pin, make sure to work with the radius slider. This lets you pick how far away you want customers from this area.

So, if you want to reach customers that are within an hour of your location, you can move the slider bar to 60 miles out. This ensures that you get the best possible reach with this feature.

Organic vs. Paid Marketing on Facebook

So far, we have spent some time talking about both organic and paid advertising on Facebook and how you can use each one. But which of these methods is actually the best one to work with?

In reality, you will need to work with both of these together to see the best results. Organic is usually the best method. This allows you to bring a lot of value to your customers, providing them with posts and information that they can actually use. And the customers who end up on your page are individuals who actually want to be there and who are interested in hearing more from you.

But there is just so much noise and competition out there, and it is hard to be heard above it all with just organic reach. Paid advertising, especially with Facebook, can help you to reach the group that you want without getting drowned out. But you need to have a good organic reach, with lots of good content, before you can even make this happen.

CHAPTER 5:

Instagram Marketing and Techniques

Instagram can be a very big mystery for a lot of companies. They want to be able to reach their target audience, and they know that working with Instagram can be the best way to make this happen in some cases. But they also may not be sure how to get started with Instagram or even the best steps to take to see results. As some companies have found out, if you are not a celebrity, it takes a lot of extra work to get famous on Instagram.

While this may be true, most companies aren't really looking to get famous. Instead, they are looking for a way to get a solid presence on the platform, a presence that will allow them to connect and engage with their target market. Instagram is a great way to showcase all of your different products through pictures, and it is growing so much every day. Finding your voice in the crowd can sometimes be a challenge. But with the tips in this chapter, you can make it happen for you.

Add Hashtags into Your Strategy

While the image that you put up on your page is very important to the success of your Instagram campaign, hashtags are one of the most important elements of your post. Captions can tell a story with the image, but the hashtag will get your image seen by those who may not be your current followers. When users on Instagram start to search for hashtags that are relevant in a specific industry, you want to make sure that your posts are one of the ones that show up. If they don't, then this means your competitors are there instead, and you are missing out.

The three main strategies that can be used for choosing hashtags:

1. Use hashtags that are pretty popular, ones that have the best chance of getting searched for. This may end up with a lot of competition, but it still increases your chances of being seen.

2. Use some hashtags that are less popular, but still highly relevant to the work that you want to do. These may drive fewer users to your posts, but the ones who find you based on these hashtags are going to be more targeted.

3. Use hashtags that are often thought to attract new followers. Some of the good ones to go with include #follow, #follow4follow, and #followme.

No matter which of the three strategies you choose to go with or even if you decide to do a little combination of each one, try to use at least one hashtag on each post. Even more hashtags can be better because it increases the amount of reach you can get on this site.

Join the Instagram Community

As you will find with all kinds of social networking, Instagram is going to work the best when you use it to form a good relationship with others. You shouldn't just go through and post pictures in your own little vacuum. It is all about participating in and forming a community around these pictures. It needs to benefit everyone, not just yourself.

There are a variety of methods that you can use to be a part of the community found on Instagram. Using things like hashtags will allow you a way to connect with many users you may not have met otherwise. Liking and commenting on pictures of other people can help you to be more engaged with the greater community. Participating in Instagram campaigns intended to help out worthy causes can make it easier for you to contribute to the greater good. And, if you share videos and images from an event, it can help your followers feel like they were in on the action.

Know How Often to Post to Get Optimal Results

There is a lot of conflicting advice out there on how often you should post on Instagram. Ultimately, only you can decide what is going to work best for your audience.

With that said, Union Metrics provides some ideas on how to test out your efforts to see what will work best when it comes to posting frequency for your business.

According to their research, which was based on monitoring 55 different brands on Instagram, Union Metrics found that most brands post about 1.5 times a day. What is more notable is that posting more often didn't result in a decreased amount of engagement.

In the past, we were told to not post on our pages too often. While you may not want to go crazy and post every hour, posting 3 or 4 times a day is not a bad thing. It isn't going to drive your customers away, and it is pretty easy to work on to make sure you are more visible. You may want to start out with just posting one time a day, and then increase the frequency slowly from there. When you notice that there is a point when engagement goes down, then you can scale back to get to your optimal level.

Have Your Images Work with Your Brand's Vibe

If you take a look on Instagram, you will notice that some of the most successful brands who pay a lot of attention to how their images are contributing to their brand identity. They have an overarching theme that comes with their images, and this theme is going to be related to the overall image of the company. This helps people to feel like they really know you when they come to your Instagram page, and they are more likely to stay around and learn more about you as time goes on.

Learn the Right Ways to Optimize the Entire Profile

It really doesn't take that long of a time for you to go through and properly optimize the profile that you are using on Instagram, but it can definitely make a big difference on how many people will actually click on your site. It can also make a difference in how they view your brand. Below are some of the tips that you can follow to help optimize your profile.

- Make sure that the description and the images on your profile go well with the vibe that you want to see in your company.

- Make sure there is always a link present that goes back to your website. You could even consider setting up a landing page that is specific for your visitors from Instagram or you can make changes to the link to help promote a current campaign or other content.

- Use the logo for the company somewhere in the profile. This lets your users know that this profile is the official one for your company.

- Consider adding at least one brand-specific hashtag to your profile. This makes it easier for your customers to know the profile belongs to you.

- If you are a local business or you have your own store, consider including your physical location into the profile as well.

- Make sure that if you have other social media profile that your images and any other content stay consistent throughout.

Understand That Growing Your Followers Can Be an Art and a Science

Without having a good solid base of followers, all of the efforts that you do on Instagram are likely to be pretty fruitless. The secret to doing this though is pretty simple: you just need to have lasting engagement because that naturally leads to followers. In other words, as you continue to post relevant and engaging images, the follower base is going to grow organically as well.

With that being said, there are a few strategies that you can use that will help to speed this process up a little bit more. Below are some of the strategies that you may want to consider using.

1. Remember that quality pictures and posts are always going to beat out quantity. If you have already started your account, make sure that you go through and edit it until only the very

best is left. No one wants to follow you if all you have is thousands of pointless images that have nothing to do with your business.

2. Always have a good and relevant caption with your pictures. Asking a question within that caption can be a good way for you to increase your engagement.

3. Be consistent. Always remember who you are posting for and remember why you are posting.

4. Use various tools like Piqura to see which images are leading you to the highest engagement, and then post more of them.

5. Engage on the photos where you interact most, and also on other profiles. As people start to see that you are interacting on a regular basis, they are going to start following you as well.

6. Make sure that if you are on Instagram, you should promote this account everywhere that you go. Promote it to other social media sites, on your physical marketing materials, and to your email subscribers.

Be a Follower (We Promise It's a Good Thing!)

Unless you go on Instagram and you are already a big name, then you won't be able to get away without following people back. And not only should you follow your own followers back, but you also need to be active in finding new users to follow. Here are several strategies that you can use to make sure you are following the right kinds of people:

1. Find some people you already know. While you are logged in to your profile, go to the profile page and click on the top right-hand corner of the screen. Then tap on the 'Find Friends' and see who is on your Facebook friends list, contacts list, and suggested users list.

2. Search for any companies or people you know by utilizing the search bar on Instagram.

3. Find people you may like to follow by using the Search and Explore feature of Instagram. You just need to click on the magnifying glass icon and then scroll down to see who is being recommended.

4. Follow influencers in the industry that you are in. Keyhole helps you to search for posts and users by hashtag, and then you can sort through the results based on how many likes they have on their posts.

5. Follow any users who are following the influencers of your industry.

6. Search for hashtags that are industry-related. This is a great way to make sure that you find targeted users in your niche.

7. You can also do a search on Google for any of the influential users in your industry. You can type in something simple like "social media" + Instagram to have this work.

Post a Lot of Engaging Videos and Photos

It is easy for you to get stuck on posting the same type of content over and over again on any social media platform that you are using. Posting product shots and selfies can be part of your repertoire, but you also need to mix things up on occasion and change up your strategy. Also, spend this time monitoring the formats that you use and seeing which ones get the most engagement. There are a ton of different post ideas that you can go with including:

- User-submitted photos
- Images and videos that are based on a holiday theme
- Day in the life shots to help show off your own personal side
- Short tutorials or demos of the product
- Simple image quotes using tools like Canva

- Sneak peeks of any new products that you have available

- Some behind the scenes photos of your employees or workspace

As you go through and try to decide what is the best for you to post, you should also consider the strategies that will help convince your followers to like and comment on them. This will ensure that you are getting the most out of your posts and can lead to more engagement with your customers.

How to Turn My Followers into Customers

Part of this chapter discussed the importance of getting followers. Followers on your profile mean that there are more eyes looking at your content and, hopefully, purchasing your products. But how do you make sure that the followers you have actually become customers, rather than just glancing at your pictures and your content on occasion? Some of the things that you can do to help turn your followers into customers include:

1. *Create some trust*: One of the biggest ways that you can turn your followers into customers is to build up trust with them. You will find that Instagram is a great way to share details about you and your business with others and doing so can help humanize your business, which then creates trust with your followers. When your

followers trust you, they are more likely to look into your services and they may choose you over the competition.

2. *Stay top of mind*: As you get more followers, actively like and comment on their posts as well. You can also use hashtags and handles which are relevant to the photos that you share and the ones you already know that the followers will search and click. Doing this will let your followers know that you are there and keep you top of mind, especially when they need you most.

3. *Make your followers feel like they are special*: When you can make your customers feel special, you will find they are more likely to follow the content that you post and more likely to work with you. To do this, give them an exclusive experience on this site, share secrets and details that aren't available on other sites, and more.

4. *Include links and calls to action*: As you share your information and posts on Instagram, make sure that each one includes a call to action and a link to your website. This makes it easier for the customer to know what you want them to do when they finish reading your post.

5. *Showcase some of the unique qualities of your business*: When you post on a consistent basis,

share more about yourself and your business, and connect well with your audience, you will find that your followers are much more loyal to you. Make sure that when you work on your Instagram profile, you create one that your followers want to be a part of, and they are more likely to become your customers.

Instagram is a great social media platform to work on. You can utilize their great picture format in order to showcase your work and the products that you are selling. When you can make a good connection with your followers and potential customers and you can create content that they really enjoy and find valuable, you will be able to get all of the customers you need from your Instagram account.

Other Tips You Can Use to Increase Your Reach with Instagram

Instagram can easily become one of the greatest tools out there to help you reach your customers and grow your business. There are currently more than 500 million users who are on Instagram each day, and this provides you with a huge pool that you can utilize for your own needs. If you want to make sure that your marketing is as good and effective as possible with Instagram, you need to make sure that you can increase your following on a consistent basis and that you keep these people around. The more people who follow you on Instagram and learn about your brand, the more people you will reach every time that you post something online.

There are a lot of things that you can do to make sure that the efforts you put into your Instagram marketing are successful. Below are some of the best tips and tricks that you may want to include in this plan:

1. Make sure to utilize all of the free tools that Instagram offers. Instagram has an option for you to create a business profile, similar to what we see with a business profile on Facebook. You can utilize this profile type to use those call to actions to get your customer to contact you or visit a certain page. You can also access various analytics about your page. Looking through these helps you to see exactly how your users are interacting with the content that you put there. You can then use this to make any of the necessary adjustments to increase follower engagement.

2. Take the time to cross-promote your post. If you would like to make sure that you can easily add the right followers to Instagram, ones who already love your brand, then you need to post across all of the social media followers on Facebook, Twitter, and more. Invite some of the followers you already have there to come onto your Instagram account. As long as you provide

them some value with doing this, you shouldn't have an issue with this one.

3. Never overwhelm your audience. You want to post enough on the page that you can keep your brand relevant, but you don't want to send out a post every five minutes either. You may have to experiment a bit in order to figure out the magic posting number that seems to work the best with you. Start with one or two times a day, and then change up the times to see what works for you.

4. Interact with your followers. Interaction is so important when it comes to being on social media, no matter which social media account you choose to go with. You can reply to the comments on your page or even do something like "Tag three of your friends who would love this!". This response can really help you to grow because it shows your customers that you are actually interested in them.

5. Pick out a hashtag that can be a bit interactive. Another idea that you may want to work with is to create a hashtag that is interactive and can create some engagement right away. A good way to do this is to make your own hashtag, and then ask any customer who actually purchases this product to post a picture of themselves

with that product, adding in that hashtag as well. This can make it easier for more people to see and hear about your business because these hashtags are going to be shared with their friends along the way.

6. Be creative when it comes to connecting with your audience. When you are creative with the images that you are using, you don't want to put up the same boring pictures day in and day out. You need to find ways to get the attention of your followers and find ways to get them to actually click on you, rather than on someone else.

When you first get started on Instagram, it may seem like you have no idea of what you are doing. But this is still a great way to reach your potential customers and can work better for your business than Facebook, Twitter, and even YouTube, as long as you can use it properly. Use the tips that we discuss in this guidebook and you will be able to rock your marketing campaign on Instagram in no time.

CHAPTER 6:

Marketing Your Business with YouTube

As a business, you will find that visual content has never been more effective or more popular, and YouTube continues to dominate when it comes to a social network that focuses on visuals. With about 85% of online adults considering themselves regular users of YouTube, the opportunities for your business to make a high-quality video and get it in front of a large and captivated audience is bigger than ever.

Why Is YouTube so Important?

YouTube is a bit different compared to some of the other social media sites that we have talked about. While Facebook is about providing good content to your customers and Instagram is more about using pictures to tell your story, YouTube spends time using videos to help you share your message with the customers you are looking for the most.

Videos are on the rise, and it is seen as one of the biggest growing media on the market. Many people are looking towards videos to get the news they want, to learn more about products, and so much more. While the other social media platforms can be used to help you reach your customers and spread some good content, they don't have the same impact as what you can get when you use videos and other visuals to your market.

YouTube is one of the best platforms to use to help you to do this. There are millions of daily users of YouTube, and, sometimes, it may seem that it is hard to reach your audience with all of the videos out there. But, if you utilize some of the other tools that you have at your disposal, such as your email list and other social media sites, you can get more followers to your YouTube page, and it won't take long before you see your page views increase.

How Can I Grow with YouTube?

YouTube is a social media site that a lot of businesses tend to avoid. They may spend some time on Facebook or Twitter or even Instagram, but if they do any videos, they simply put one or two on their websites and link back to the other social media sites they have. They forget the power that can come behind working on YouTube to reach customers and the competitive advantage they can get from doing this.

YouTube actually can present you with a ton of ways to help you grow your business, no matter what kind of business or industry that you are in. Below are some of the biggest ways that YouTube will help you see some major growth in your business:

1. *Visual media gets more customers*: You will find that content, especially visual content, is going to make a big difference in the response that you get from your customers. Humans are visual creatures. When you can create engaging videos, you can appeal to the passive learning aspect of human behavior and can really appeal to your visual nature.

2. *Tutorials and testimonials*: The best company videos are the ones that can share information, and even resources, on how your services and products can perform for the customer. These videos could also include some great testimonials from the current or previous customers. These video testimonials make these accounts more tangible and can have a big effect on the prospects you have.

3. *Working with a playlist*: These playlists make it easier to create a nice list of videos that your viewers can check out in a series. This can make it easier for related content to be organized together, can guide users through a series of tutorials that you have, and more.

4. *Feedback and comments*: YouTube will provide you with a commenting system that lets people

post some feedback on your videos. This provides you with a tremendous opportunity to interact with your potential customers and can even alleviate any concerns or questions right off the bat.

5. *Video social network*: Even though YouTube is basically a website to put a lot of videos on, it is also seen as a social network site just like the rest of them we have talked about. It gives the user the ability to interact and engage as they want to with your brand, and it is a good way for you to build up a following with some of the users who are already on it.

6. *YouTube ads*: You can also choose to work with some paid options for advertising in order to get the most out of your YouTube page. By leveraging the YouTube ads that you have, it is easier to budget the money that you need to get the right traction in the early stages or to make sure that you provide a boost needed to your more mature profile.

7. *Customization*: YouTube provides you with some options so that you can add customizations to your page or your channel. This is a good way for you to integrate your business branding in with your profile and your channel so customers can get even more familiar with you.

8. SEO: One nice thing about YouTube is that it is set up to work with Google. This means that you can perform some SEO on your videos, and if you pick the right keywords and start ranking high enough, your videos will start showing up in Google searches.

These are just a few of the benefits that you can get when it comes to working on your own YouTube channel. This is definitely a social media platform that a lot of businesses miss out on because they don't even think about it to begin with. But if you can provide fresh content on a regular basis to your customers, you will find that it is easier than ever to really reach your customers in new and innovative ways.

How Do I Interact with Other People on My Channel?

One of the most important things that you can do when you want to work on YouTube is that you need to interact with others. It is never a good idea to make a video, then post it up for others to see without ever making any comments or interacting with others who come and view or comment on your video. You may get a few views here or there, but it will start looking pretty superficial if people get on your channel and there never is any interaction from you.

This doesn't mean that you have to spend all day long on your computer waiting for a comment to appear. But it means that you should check in on a regular basis and respond and interact. Even spending a few minutes each day can be enough to make this happen. Your customers will appreciate the time you take to comment or reply back or even to answer some of the questions that they may have.

The more interaction you can add into the channel, the better. If someone comments on one of your videos, then make sure that you comment back to them, at least as much as you can. Over time, you will hopefully have a ton of followers and views, and it can be hard to reply to everything, but do the best that you can.

Just like with the other social media platforms, you also need to search around and find other places to respond and comment on as well. You can look through other videos in your industry and leave comments as well. Make sure that these comments are well thought out and that they make sense for the video that you just watched. If you do this properly, you will find that it can really help your business to grow as more and more people will notice your comments or your advice and will head over to your videos as well.

All About the Videos

When it comes to using YouTube, it is all about the videos. You need to fill up your channel with videos that are high-quality, informative and full of value to the customer. Having a lot of videos that meet these criteria can help you to extend your reach. Having a lot of videos just for the sole purpose of having a ton of videos is going to turn your customers off.

There are a few things that you can remember about posting the type of videos that you post. First, you need to come up with a good posting schedule that you can stick with. Your customers will rely on a good posting schedule. If they know that you always upload a video on Thursday evening, then they know the exact time to come back and look for something new. This is a great way to build up anticipation, and as more and more people talk about the video, it will be nice to have that steady timeframe for them to check in at.

You can choose any posting time that works the best for you. Just make sure that it is something that you can stick with and remain consistent with. If you are worried about not being able to get the video done each week on time, consider creating a few videos at a time and then having them ready to go anytime that you might fall behind.

Another thing that you must always have with each and every video you post is high quality. There are millions of videos found on YouTube, and many of them are done by professionals. If you want your business to be taken seriously in this market, then you must make sure that your videos are of the highest quality possible.

What this means is that you shouldn't have a video that looks like a home video or like something an amateur can do. If you don't have the resources or the experience to do it yourself, consider hiring a professional videographer to do the work. They can work on each video and make sure that it looks professional, that the videos are consistent and look good together, and that you get them uploaded in a timely manner.

The information that is inside of the videos also needs to be informative and provide some kind of value to your customers. Just making a video because it is that time of the week isn't going to help your business to grow. You need to have videos that teach your customers something, that let them know something new or provide value in some other way.

If you can, try to make a video that can go viral. This is really hard to do because often it is a surprise which videos are going to become viral. But if you can come up with a video idea that is going to catch the attention of a bunch of people, that will get them to share it a bunch as well. Doing this can help you to reach a ton of new people, many of whom may have never even heard about your business before but could become loyal followers and customers once they see the video. Take a look on YouTube and other sources and see what videos have become viral hits, and then try to see how you can adapt that to work for your industry as well.

And finally, no matter what kind of video you choose to work with—there are a ton of options (look at the next chapter to see some ideas)—you must make sure that you always have a call to action at the end. When the customer is done watching the video, what is it that you are hoping they will do? Do you want them to check out your website? Do you want them to like your video or look at some of the other videos that you have? Do you want them to make a purchase? You have to decide what you would like the customer to do, and then provide this in the call to action at the end of your video.

Working on YouTube can be a great experience. Visual content is becoming a huge marketing tool, one that will change the way that many businesses reach their customers and make sales. Being able to reach your customers with high-quality and valuable videos can often set you apart from your competition. In the next few chapters, we will take a closer look at some of the ways that you can market your brand or your business on YouTube, using both organic and paid advertising to help you out.

CHAPTER 7:

Organic YouTube Marketing

If you have been toying with the idea of marketing your business through YouTube but you aren't sure where you should start or what you need to do, then this chapter is the one that you really need to read. Every business can benefit from using YouTube to promote themselves, and staying up-to-date on how it works, creating videos that your customers will find valuable, and learning how to reach the right people can make a big difference in how well you can use YouTube to help your business grow. Some of the different marketing tips that we will look at for YouTube include:

- Ways to optimize the videos that you create for searches and clicks

- The best types of videos for you to create and then have your customers share

- Ways to promote your videos, as well as your channel as a whole

- Ways to use paid YouTube ads to get your reach to extend as far as possible

How to Optimize Your Video to Get the Most Searches and Clicks

If you want to be successful on YouTube, you must make sure that you optimize all of your videos to work well with both Google and YouTube. By using the right keywords in your title, tags, and description can make it easier for your customers to find you if they do a search on you.

To start with is the title. Google often recommends that you use your keyword first, and then the branding second; this is to make it more SEO-friendly. You could also use season and episode numbers if that is relevant, but make sure this is at the end. The title that you create for your video should paint a clear picture of what the viewer is going to see if they click on your videos. Ideally, you will keep the title to 50 characters or less. You can make it longer, but often a title that is longer than this is going to be hard to read through, and this actually decreases the chances of someone clicking on your page.

You can also work with tags. These are going to be the main keywords that you want to have related to your video. Many people believe that YouTube is going to put the most weight on the first couple tags that you list out, so make sure that you rank your keywords with the most important ones near the front. If you can, try to use all 120 characters, but don't just put random keywords down if they don't relate to your video.

Next, you need to work with your description. You always want to make sure that there is a call to action so that your viewers can take the next step. This can include something like getting them to watch another video or click on your link. Then, the first few sentences will be displayed in search results, so make sure it has your value proposition there, maybe with a few important keywords in it as well.

Also, make sure to add in some high-quality thumbnails to help the viewer. When viewers are scrolling through the search results for YouTube, you may find that the right thumbnail can influence whether they decide to click on your video or not. The optimal size for these images would be 1280 px x 720 px. You could have YouTube automatically generate a thumbnail for you, but it is always best for you to create and upload your own thumbnail.

What Types of Videos Should I Create and Share?

Just because you can upload a ton of videos to YouTube, doesn't mean that you should upload anything and everything that you can find. You need to make sure that you are creating and sharing high-quality videos, ones that actually showcase the products that you want to sell and will provide value to your customers.

One of the biggest questions that business owners will ask when they are considering marketing on YouTube is what types of videos they should consider posting. The prospect of coming up with the best ideas for making engaging and entertaining videos that also help you to make more sales can be hard. There are a lot of different kinds of videos that you can choose to go with to market on YouTube including:

1. *Tutorials*: These videos show your viewer how they should perform a certain task.

2. *Product demos*: These demonstrate some of the common uses for your products.

3. *Testimonials from customers*: You can make videos where you interview customers who were satisfied in the past. You can also share a user-generated testimonial on your own channel.

4. *Intro video for your business*: YouTube will allow you to create what is known as a Chanel Trailer, where you can welcome all new viewers to your business. You can use this to provide a brief introduction to your business, letting the viewers know what kinds of videos they should expect to see if they decide to subscribe to this channel.

5. *Behind-the-scene videos*: You can even choose to take your viewers on a tour of your workspace or your office. If you have other employees, consider introducing the viewers to them.

6. *Tips and tricks*: If you have any, it is a good idea to provide some insights that will help your viewers and your prospects.

7. *Live presentations*: Any time that you can go live, you are providing a great service to your customers and really getting them interested. If you ever go and speak at a tradeshow or a conference, make sure to record and share this on your YouTube page.

8. *Webinars*: Most webinar software providers make it easy for you to record your webinars. You can then upload these to your YouTube channel and share with your audience.

9. *Commercials*: You can easily put your commercials on YouTube as well. If you need some ideas for the types of ads that work well on YouTube, check out Always and Old Spice.

10. *Product launches*: If you have a new product coming out to the market soon, share the release of this with some of your YouTube users so they know the news.

As you go through and create and promote different video types, it won't take long to learn the type that your audience seems to respond the best too. This will help you to target your advertisements to the audience you want to reach and can help you to make the content that works the best for your business.

How to Promote Your Videos as Well as Your YouTube Channel

The next thing we need to look at when it comes to organically reach with your videos is the different methods of how you can promote your videos and your channels. There are three main ways to get more views for the videos that you are creating and adding to your channel which include:

1. Getting a higher rank for YouTube or Google keyword searches
2. Having a large subscriber base on YouTube
3. Promoting your channel and your videos through other web properties

The previous section already took some time to discuss the best ways to optimize the videos that you are working on. Growing your channel on YouTube and being able to promote these channels and videos on other web properties that you own will be the next, and, sometimes, it is the most challenging part of this whole process. Some of the ways that you can help increase your views and subscribers to your videos include:

1. *Promote these videos and your YouTube channel on the other social media profiles*: You should include some hashtags that are relevant to these posts so that you get even more reach.

2. *Engage with your loyal fans*: When you spend time looking through the Creator Dashboard, you will see which users are the most engaged with the content you provide. You can consider involving these fans in some way to nurture some brand ambassador relationships later on.

3. *Add a widget for YouTube on your blog*: You can use a tool such as Tint to help you display a number of videos—can be your own or someone else's—in a widget that goes right on your blog or website.

4. *Collaborate with other business owners who run a complimentary niche*: Approach some other YouTubers and see if they are willing to promote your videos if you promote theirs. You can even consider co-branding videos to use them for both audiences.

5. *Engage with your users, both on their videos and on yours*: Social media sees the best results when you interact and engage with others users, but this doesn't mean that you should just stay on your own channel. Leave comments that are thought out well on videos and respond to any comments left on yours. Remember, the more interactions you have with your videos, the higher you will rank in the search.

6. *Share your videos on your email list*: Direct the audience to your embedded videos on your site to increase your page views and your video views.

7. *Embed the videos onto your blog or website*: Add videos to existing posts on your blog or you can even come up with new blog posts that are specifically there to promote your videos. This will help you to increase your video views and increase your page views on the site.

Making your reach organic on YouTube can take some time and may not happen as quickly as you would like. But, it is a great way to ensure that you are finding people who are truly interested in the content that you try to provide. There are also some paid options that you can choose to work with as well, but whether these are going to be as successful as the organic reach that we have just talked about, it depends on your audience, on the products that you are trying to sell, and more.

CHAPTER 8:

Paid YouTube Marketing

Just like with some of the other social networks that we have talked about, there are ways to use YouTube and extend the reach of your content in a manner that is much faster than organic reach. YouTube ads will allow you to turn any of the videos that you have into an ad for your business. When you do this, it makes sure that your video is going to be seen before other videos when a potential viewer types in keywords related to your business. This can also be used to have your video show up alongside other videos that YouTube users are watching at the time, if they relate to the topics in your video.

There are several different targeting options that you can use when you set up YouTube ads. You can target based on things like location, gender, age, keywords, and more. You can also choose the size of your ad. Some people will choose to go with a large masthead that is somewhere between 850 by 250 or the smaller standard display ads that are either 300 by 250 or 300 by 600.

Using YouTube ads can be a good way for you to make sure that the videos you produce get a nice boost. For someone who is just getting started on YouTube, these ads can help you to get off the ground and can increase your social proof, which can include things like comments, views, and thumbs up.

There are many different options that you can choose to work within YouTube marketing when it comes to paid advertising, but the YouTube ads are usually the most commonly used one. If you are going to pick a video to advertise, make sure that you pick a high-quality video, one that has the potential to go viral and one that is likely to get people back to your channel to watch more videos or to make a purchase.

You have to be careful when you choose to work with YouTube ads. While it can provide you with a ton of benefits for your business and can bring more viewers and potential customers back to your page, you have to make sure that you are picking out good videos, and that you are providing value to your customers. Here are some of the best practices that you must keep in mind as a business owner who wants to use YouTube ads to increase their reach:

1. Make sure that when you create or pick out a video for this, the first few seconds act as a hook. This hook is what you need to real the viewers in to watch the rest of the video. If you cannot capture the attention of the viewer in the first 5 seconds, then they are not going to stick around. Figure out what is your most

captivating content first, and then back this up with the details and facts later in the video.

2. Keep the ads short and sweet. Most experts on YouTube recommend that if you are going to make a video ad, keep it to one minute or less. Unbounce found that about 80% of your viewers are going to click out of the ad after a minute anyway, making it too long is just going to be a waste of your time. Shorter video ads are very important when using this service.

3. Focus on the goals of the advertisement, rather than on the views. While it is important to have some on-site engagement, and this can be a great indicator that the video is hitting the marks that you want with your viewers, take a look at whether or not your YouTube ads are helping you meet your specific goals. Are these views resulting in more conversions or even sending the right kind of traffic to your site? If the answer is no, then it is time to make some adjustments.

4. Make sure there is a call to action in your video. We have mentioned this a bit before, but it is important to always have a call to action present in every video, especially in your advertisements. This helps to increase the amount of engagement that you are getting from your customers. If you

are working with the TrueView ads (we will bring these up in a bit), you can choose if you would like to overlay the call to action over the ad, ensuring that viewers are going to see this call to action right when they see the video start.

5. Before you record the video for the ad, always have a goal in mind. What are you hoping to get people to do when they are done watching the ad? Do you want them to visit your website? Do you want them to follow your channel? Do you want them to call your business? Do you want them to purchase something? Having this specific goal in mind ahead of time will make it easier to monitor the effectiveness of these ads.

6. Consider video remarketing to get more engagement: Remarketing, which is sometimes called retargeting, will allow you a chance to target these ads to users who interacted with your YouTube channel or videos in the past. This makes it easier for you to achieve a positive return on investment for any ads that you want to make on YouTube.

As you spend your investment on a marketing strategy for YouTube, remember to focus on the content and what you put into your video before you even think about starting a marketing campaign to go with it. With more than 300 hours of video being added to YouTube each minute, you know that the playing field on this site is crowded and you must make sure that all of your videos can speak to your audience and provide them with value for it to succeed. Then, once you have had the time to create a video that meets all of these criteria, you will be able to promote and distribute it through all of the channels that you have, and then add in some paid promotion as well.

Working with TrueView

One thing to consider when you are ready to do paid advertising with YouTube, you will hear about TrueView InStream ads. These are basically the way that YouTube is going to create commercials similar to what you may see when watching your favorite shows on live television. This is one of the most successful forms of online advertising that YouTube can offer to businesses.

When you decide to take out a TrueView ad, you are going to create a short video for your channel or brand, one that can encourage potential customers to learn more about your company. These are the ads that will show up at the beginning of a monetized video, but if there are some videos that are longer in length, these ads can show up in the middle of them as well.

However, if there is a video on YouTube that is non-monetized, there will never be ads that show up on it. If you would like to see your commercial show up on a specific channel, make sure that you check and see if that channel is monetized before you go any further. If it is, you can set up the ad to be shown on those videos. If it isn't, then you will have to do something else.

Another way that you can work with TrueView is with their InDisplay ads. These are going to show up as a thumbnail next to a video that someone is watching at that time. These will sometimes look like the PPC ads you see from other sources, but they have a thumbnail next to them. People will then be able to choose when and if they click on your ads. These ads are sometimes used to promote other videos that you created and put on your channel. These InDisplay ads can also be a good way for you to jump start or even restart a viral campaign.

There are a lot of different options that you can utilize when it comes to TrueView, and you can be a bit creative to stand out from the crowd. You will notice though that when you use some of these TrueView ads, you are not going to be billed in the same manner that you are for a regular AdWords ad that you would place with Google.

InStream ads are going to be billed on a cost per view format. This means that you will be charged any time someone clicks on your ad and then stays there for a minimum of 30 seconds. If this happens, regardless of the conversion or not, you will have to pay. If the viewer doesn't click on the ad or they don't stay for the 30 seconds, then you won't have to pay for that.

Keep in mind that a lot of YouTube ads are going to allow your potential viewer to skip the ad after only 3 seconds has passed if they are using either a desktop or mobile device. This could be good news for you. If someone happens to see your brand for 3 seconds or even slightly longer then skips the commercial, they could potentially head to your YouTube channel later on to learn some more about you. If they make a purchase and more, then you got a potential customer without having to pay for them.

The InDisplay ads that we talked about before are going to be a cost per view format as well. You will be charged any time that a potential customer clicks on your video's thumbnail and starts to watch the video on their watch page. If the customer sees your ad and doesn't click on it, then you won't be charged for that view. But if the customer clicks on it and watches it even for a short amount of time, then you will be charged for that customer.

These are the two main options that you can use when you want to do paid advertising on YouTube. The way that you become more effective with YouTube marketing is to create a good video, one that sets you apart from the competition and all of the other videos that are found on YouTube. This may mean that you need to focus more on the video that you are creating so that you can really entice the customer and to ensure that your YouTube paid promotions are as effective as possible.

A Few Words About Remarketing Your YouTube Viewers

One neat thing that you can do is show a personalized ad to millions of viewers all across YouTube and other partner sites based on how they interacted with your channel or your videos in the past. This is known as a process of video remarketing. By reinforcing your message to those who have already gone through and seen your channel or your videos, you will find even more success with a better return on investment since these viewers showed interested in your products or videos in the past.

There are a lot of great benefits that can come from using YouTube remarketing. Some of these benefits include:

- *A better return on investment*: Advertisers who use remarketing on YouTube have been able to improve their return on investment. This is because they are showing these videos to people who already showed some interest in the product or the service.

- *Broader scope*: With the big YouTube network, it is possible that your video ad will reach a lot of potential customers, all of whom are on the remarketing list.

- *Efficient pricing*: The Google Ads auction model that you will use for these is going to provide you with some competitive rates to help meet the return on investment that you want. With the CPV bidding, you are going to pay for views on the video and some other types of interactions with the video, such as the call to action overlays, clicks on the video, cards, and companion banners.

- *Flexibility*: You will find that website remarketing, which can also be known as retargeting or remessaging, will be based on the actions of the visitor on your website. You can go through and remarket based on the actions that are specific to your YouTube videos, including things like when viewers like, dislike, comment on, and share your video.

So, how does this whole process work? Remarketing lists can be created when you take the time to link together your Google Ads and your YouTube channel account. Once you have a chance to link these accounts, you can create your own remarketing lists, ones that will reach the customers and people who have done the following YouTube related actions:

- Shared a video from your channel

- Commented on a video from your channel
- Added any video from your channel to a playlist
- Linked any video from your channel
- Visited a channel page
- Took the time to subscribe to your channel
- Viewed certain videos as an ad
- Viewed any video as an ad from a channel
- Viewed certain videos
- Viewed any video from a channel

You can then use these lists when you are looking through the settings for targeting for new or existing campaigns. You can always go through and manage your lists any time that you need, simply by selecting the Shared library and then Audiences if you are using the previous ads experience or the Audience manager if you are now using the new Google Ads experience. One thing to note here is that you cannot make these remarketing lists from any of the views you get on your bumper ads.

There are several best practices that you can try to use when it comes to doing a remarketing campaign. You are already marketing to people who have shown some interest in your business or your products, so that is a good start in the beginning. But you also want to make sure that you get the best return on investment with your remarketing lists. Below are some of the features that you should explore in order to make this happen:

- *Try out different formats for your ad*: You can build and then target the remarketing campaign that you are doing with various video ads along with other creative formats that are available, including rich media ads, images, and text.

- *Engage with your mobile customers*: Mobile advertising is growing like crazy and more and more of your potential customers will find you through their mobile devices. You can work with square and vertical videos to make it easier to engage with these customers when they find you on the YouTube app.

- *Detailed reports*: You can optimize your remarketing campaign based on performance metrics. You could choose to raise bids on certain channels or specific topics, for example, which help you generate the best response to your ads.

- *Ease of use*: You should make sure that you are creating, managing, and targeting these remarketing lists as best as possible.

- *Custom audiences*: You even get the option of customizing your targeting by combining your remarketing lists together and seeing what happen. For example, you could reach audiences who viewed your movie trailer, but maybe hadn't seen the ad that promoted the release of the DVD.

Remarketing is just one of the ways that you can market your business on YouTube. It is often seen as one of the most effective methods though because it allows you to reach your customers, especially those who already viewed your content in the past. These customers are more likely to be interested in your business or in your product compared to others, and targeting them in these campaigns can really make a difference in the conversions you get.

CHAPTER 9:

Using Twitter to Grow Your Business

The next social media site that we are going to look at is Twitter. With more than 313 million active users each month and a demographic that is young too, Twitter can be a great place for you to market yourself and see some great results. And you will find that it is pretty easy to set up your own Twitter profit. You just need to come up with your own handle (the name of your profile), upload a good picture to be your profile picture, fill out a bio, and send out the first tweet, and you are ready to go. There are more steps to growing the account, but these simple steps will at least help you to get yourself started.

Growing a real following through Twitter can take some more work than just sending out tweets when you have a big event or a new product. Twitter is useful because it helps you to engage with your audience and actually interact with them. This isn't going to happen if you just send out a few tweets a year. Let's take a closer look at Twitter and how it can help you grow your business.

How Is Twitter Different from the Rest?

The approach that you have to each social media site that you work with should be a bit different. You won't be able to use the same strategy that you do with Twitter as you do with your Facebook marketing plan. It is important that you learn more about the way Twitter works and the best way to use it to get the best benefits.

There are many different ways that a business can utilize Twitter to reach their needs. Some of the main ways include:

- Managing their reputation
- Branding themselves
- Networking so they can find other similar businesses and potential customers in the industry
- Interacting with their customers and potential customers
- Driving engagement for some of the promotional activities that they are working on
- Sharing the content and information that they have about their business and about their products

Just like with all of the other social media sites that we have talked about, most of these activities have something to do with interactions. It is not just about broadcasting out your content, like what can happen with Pinterest and Instagram sometimes. Twitter works because of open communication.

Now that we know a bit about the importance of Twitter and how businesses will often use it, it is time to go into some of the things that you need to know in order to get started with marketing on Twitter. We will go beyond the how to for setting up a good profile. We will look at some of the real strategies that will ensure you can reach your customers and that you won't waste your time through this platform.

Finding Your Untapped Market Through Twitter Chats

Many marketers have started to ask how they can get more followers on Twitter. But the real question that should be done here is how do you get more active Twitter followers? As any business knows, just because you have a bunch of followers doesn't mean that they are interacting with you or even seeing the things that you are posting. If you have 100 followers but only 5 of them are active and seeing your posts, that isn't such a good thing.

The answer to this problem is Twitter chats. These chats have been pushed for a bit of time, but many marketers have been slow to try them out and see what power they can get out of them. But as more people try them, the popularity is growing. Getting into these chats now could be a great way for you to see some results with finding not just followers, but active followers on Twitter.

The reason that this tool is so effective is that people who use them are the ones who already are active on Twitter. You aren't going to find inactive users on the platform. They won't just use it to distribute or consume content. Instead, these people are on Twitter and using it for the purpose it was designed for, which is to interact. These followers are great because they are the ones who will reply to the Tweet you put up, they will retweet your content, and they can help you spread your message.

When you are ready to start on Twitter chats, make sure you look for some that are in your related industry. There are a lot of Twitter chat groups so make sure to find one that will work for your needs and your industry. But if you find there aren't any options for you, then you can start out your own. Either way, the key to seeing some success with Twitter chats is to ensure that you are more than a spectator. You must be there, interacting and adding value along with others, or this trick won't work for you at all.

Always Plan Ahead

Never wait until a big event or even a big holiday before you start planning out some of your posts. For example, by late September or early October, you should already have your tweets and content ready to go live for Halloween. When November comes, you should have some tweets ready for Thanksgiving and then on to Christmas.

Taking the time to plan ahead of the holidays and any other special events that occur in your company can ensure that you have plenty of time. You can use this to pick out trending hashtags for your topics and create some high-quality content without feeling rushed.

Instead of waiting until a few days before, you should make it your goal to come up with a campaign not later than 2 weeks before the scheduled time. There are also various calendars that you can find online that will help you look at the upcoming holidays so you can make a comprehensive plan of what you want to write your tweet for.

Once that special day comes up, whether it is Halloween, Christmas, Thanksgiving, or some other day, you can then follow any of the trending hashtags for that event. You can also choose to send out content as events are happening, rather than waiting until the momentum is done to get it up and working. This is one of the benefits of working with Twitter.

Make Sure That Your Tweets Are Always Conversational

Remember that Twitter is similar to your other social media sites in that you need to interact and have a conversation with the people you are talking to on the site. Often, this is something forgotten, and then they wonder why they aren't seeing the results that they were looking for when they got started on this social media site.

The way that many different companies look at Twitter and the way they decide to tweet is going to be very one dimensional. These companies will write out tweets that are just broadcasts, which is not really what Twitter should be about. Your Tweets are not headlines with a link like a newspaper. They shouldn't just be funny statements or inspirational quotes either. Instead, they need to be able to open up the door for a lot of conversation and communication between you and your customers.

The good news is that you don't have to just use your personal account to engage with their customers. It is easy for a business to benefit from this kind of personalization in the communication that they provide to their customers. Some of the tips that you can use to make this all happen includes:

1. Make some of your tweets questions to your followers, rather than just posting news all of the time.

2. Try to get about 30-40% of your tweets into replies to other people.

3. When you want to add a link into your tweet, add in at least a line of your own insight. This helps to spark the conversation a bit more and will make it more likely that others will respond to your tweet.

4. You should try to tweet directly to the audience. Instead of writing out something like "Blog Post Title" and then a link, you could ask a question like "What do you all think of this new post?" to help get others to interact a bit more.

Taking the time and effort to be a bit more conversational on your tweets can mean a higher amount of engagement. And over the long term, this is going to result in more activity for your Twitter account as a whole. And when you are more active and more responsive, it could result in a lot of new customers, and that can help your bottom line.

Create a Good Tweeting Strategy and Schedule

This one is similar to planning ahead, but it can be used all throughout the year, rather than just at big events. For this one, you should have a set posting schedule that works for your Twitter account. This tweeting schedule should take the time to detail when and what you plan to tweet on your page. The number of times that you decide to tweet will vary based on your goals and what seems to work the best for your business. Some people will do a tweet once a day, while others may find that doing it 3 times seems to work the best for them and their customers.

This strategy can list out the times you are going to post, and you can even write out the posts that you want to have show up on the profile ahead of time. This strategy can also take some time to outline things like when you are going to link something in a tweet, when you are going to release a new product, when you are going to share information, and more.

You should include all of this as a part of an overall content strategy. This is important if you publish your content through many platforms such as Twitter, Facebook, and a blog. This strategy is going to be so important and ensures that people see the things that you want them to.

For example, you must ensure that your customers are seeing the link to your blog or your product more than one time. There is a chance that they will miss out on it the first time or maybe forgot about it. If you just post the link one time, then you are missing out on a lot of potential customers. With your Twitter planning strategy, you can make sure that you get the post link listed more than once so that you have a better chance of reaching your potential customers and you don't end up not posting more than once.

Twitter Video

While Twitter is not always the first option that people will think about when they want to get started with video marketing, this is still something that you can consider adding into your Twitter marketing campaign. Twitter may not be as advanced with video marketing as you will see with YouTube, but it gives you a few options that can be helpful when you want to promote using videos on this site.

The first option is to use the native video feature that is already available through Twitter. This feature is going to allow you to record videos that are up to 140 seconds long. When these videos are done, you can upload these straight to the stream on your Twitter profile. If you want to make things easier and your videos is going to be about 2 minutes or less, then this option can be a great one to choose. If you would like to do something a bit longer or you would like some more features to use, then you may want to go with the second option.

Another option that you can go with when you use Twitter is Periscope. This is a live streaming app that Twitter actually owns. Periscope can integrate your content into Twitter, which means that if you do a live stream, this is going to show up on the Twitter feeds for your followers. Then, when the stream is over, that recording will still sit around so your viewers can watch it whenever is the most convenient for them.

The second option can be nice because you get the chance of going live. This attracts more attention from your potential customers because they can watch you, ask you questions, and so much more. Add in the fact that these live videos were able to get more than 31 million views in 2016, and more as time has gone on, it is definitely worth your time to add at least a few of these videos onto your Twitter feed on occasion.

Set Some Goals and Some Milestones

No type of marketing campaign is going to be complete if you don't have some measurable goals that you would like to see done at a certain point. Without these goals, objectives, and milestones, you may as well quit now. This is because you are setting yourself up to make the same mistakes that other companies are going to fall into when they decide it is time to work on their own social media marketing, whether it is with Twitter or other sites.

In fact, at least 41% of companies state that they really don't know if their efforts in social media are working or not. This is never a good thing because it means that these many companies are wasting money without knowing if they are being successful or not. A big reason that many companies feel this way is that they aren't really keeping good track of their activities, and they aren't setting the right objectives that are needed to see success.

What most businesses do instead is just publish some content on one of their social media accounts, and then they just publish some content in the hopes that it will do something to help the brand without having any plan to go with it, and then praying it will not work well with Twitter. The first option here is to set up the goals and the objectives that you want to see when you are on Twitter. Some of the different objectives that you may want to consider for your business include:

- Build up a following that is engaged
- Monitor and then find ways to improve the reputation of your brand
- Network with other bloggers, as well as the influencers, who are found in your industry
- Try to drive some more traffic over to your website
- Find ways to get more leads
- Respond to any of the complaints that you get from the customer as quickly as possible

You have to choose the objectives that seem to work best for your needs. You won't be able to work on all of these at once. But picking out one at a time to improve can make a big difference. Once you have your objective picked out, you will then need to establish some accomplishments that will be able to tie in with those objectives. Some of the things that may work for this and can help you measure how well your objective is being followed and accomplished includes the following:

1. Add in a minimum of 100 new contacts to your Twitter page.

2. Improve the referrals that you get out of Twitter by at least 30 percent.

3. Generate a minimum of 20 leads from the posts that you do on Twitter.

4. Make sure that your response time is under 10 minutes (or another time frame that works for your business).

5. Keep the response rate to your customers over 90%. This means that you are going to interact with customers, as many as possible, so they know you are there and paying attention.

6. Increase the amount of retweets and @mentions by 15 percent.

And before we finish here, make sure that all of the goals you set have a very specific deadline. You could set it for a week, a month, a quarter, or whatever tends to work the best for you. This helps you to determine if the strategy is working well for you, and if you need to make any adjustments.

Paid Advertising on Twitter

Just like with the other social media sites, you have the option of doing paid advertising with Twitter. Twitter ads are great for helping you get a good message out in front of the users, the ones who are the most likely to show some interest in your brand and in your products. According to data provided by Twitter, ad engagement has increased by 69%, while the cost per ad engagement has dropped by 28%. Add in that there are new ad formats that you can choose from with Twitter, and it is the perfect time for you to try running a Twitter ad for yourself.

There are a lot of different options that you can choose from when it comes to Twitter ads. Some of the best options that you can choose from include:

1. *Promoted Tweets*

    These types of tweets are simply tweets that you are going to pay to get displayed to people on Twitter who are not following you yet. They can work just like regular tweets in that others can comment on them, like them, and even retweet them as they like. They will also look like regular tweets in many cases, other than they will have a Promoted label on them.

    These tweets are going to appear on the users' timeline or on their profile, near the top of search results, and even on the desktop and mobile apps for Twitter. This is a great way to discuss your brand and let new potential followers know more about you. If you are careful with the way that you set these up and you make them really informative and valuable, it is likely that you will get a ton of interactions. The more interactions, the more people who will see the advertisement and the easier it will be for you to get new followers.

2. *Promoted Accounts*

Another option that you can work with is a promoted account. These are sometimes known as Followers campaign. They will make it easier for you to promote the account you are using for business to targeted users who aren't following you yet, but who may find some of your content interesting. This can be a great way to find people who are already interested in topics in your industry, so they are more likely to start following you.

These accounts will show up on the timelines of those people you follow. They can also show up in the Who to Follow suggestions and search results. They will list out that they have been promoted, but they will also have a Follow button on them, so your potential customers have a chance to click and start following your page.

3. *Promoted Trends*

When you see that a topic is trending on Twitter, it means that it is one of the most talked about subjects. It also is a topic that is going to appear on the timeline of different users, on their Explore tab, and on the Twitter app. If you do a promoted trend, you will be able to promote a hashtag of your choice at the top of this list so it gains a lot more visibility.

When a user decides to click on this promoted trend, they are going to see an organic list of search results on that topic. What is different here though is that Promoted Tweet from your business will be the very first option at the top of this list. As people start to pick up on this specific hashtag and they decide to use it for their own tweets, you will start to gain more organic exposure which will increase the reach that you are able to get for your campaign.

One thing to keep in mind when you want to do a promoted trend is that these are not going to be available for any business or advertisers who are doing the self-serve options on Twitter.

4. *Automated Ads*

If you are pretty new to the whole idea of advertising on social media and you are a little unsure about what you should do or even how much you can spend or your marketing team is small and doesn't have a lot of available time, then working with Twitter Promote Mode may be the best option for you.

If you choose to go with Twitter Promote Mode, it is going to cost you about $99 USD each month. When you turn it on, the first ten tweets that you do for that day will automatically be promoted over to the audience that you have selected, as long as this selected audience passes the quality filter from Twitter. Replies, quote tweets, and retweets are never going to be promoted. You will also get a Promoted Account campaign that is ongoing.

You need to go through a bit and make some adjustments and add in the different specifications that you want. For example, you have to write out the tweets that you want to use, the audience that you would like to target, and more. According to estimates that Twitter gives, accounts that work with Twitter Promote Mode can reach about 30,000 additional people and gain an average of 30 new followers each month.

As you can see, there are a number of different benefits that come with working on Twitter. Twitter is a great way for you to promote your business and open up communication with your customers in a way that just isn't found with other sites. Rather than just posting information (although you can do this on occasion), you will spend time in conversations with your customers, interacting with them, and more. Twitter can be a great idea to implement into your marketing campaign to get the most out of reaching your customers.

Conclusion

Thanks for making it through to the end of *Social Media Marketing Secrets*. Let's hope it was informative and able to provide you with all of the tools you need to achieve your goals whatever they may be.

The next step is to use the information that we discussed in this guidebook to create your own social media marketing plan. There are so many benefits that come with having a presence on at least a few different social media sites. These sites are where a ton of your customers are right now, and not taking advantage of them simply means you are letting your competition beat you. This guidebook tells you all of the secrets and tips that you need to get started with your own social media marketing campaign.

In this guidebook, we had taken some time to talk about the top names in social media, namely Facebook, Instagram, YouTube, and Twitter. All of these can help you to reach your customers and see great results, as long as you are willing to put in the work and as long as you understand how each platform works. This guidebook spent time looking at each one in more depth and explored some of the marketing strategies that you can use to make each one work. There are also other social media sites that you may have interest in and figuring out the one that meets with your audience and where they like to spend time, and you can use some of the same tips to help you out there.

Social media should be a part of any business's marketing plan. There are so many customers who spend a good amount of time on social media, and this is a great way to build trust and interact with your customers to turn them into purchasers. Make sure to read through this guidebook and learn more about the best social media marketing tips.

Finally, if you found this book useful in any way, a review on Amazon is always appreciated!

The New York Litigators: The Rights Stuff Attorneys of the Legal Profession

Michael Boyajian

Copyright © 2019 Michael Boyajian

ISBN: 9781792825286

Jera Studios Publishing

The New York Litigators: The
Attorneys of the Legal Professi

Michael Boyajian

Jera Studios Publishing

I dedicate this book to the Court Street attorney, past, present and future and to my wife Jeri my life partner in my law career.

Contents

Oaths 7
Rules of Professional Responsibility 9
Chapter One 11
Chapter Two 21
Chapter Three.. 27
Chapter Four.. 41
Chapter Five... 51
Chapter Six... 61
Chapter Seven 77
Chapter Eight... 81
Chapter Nine.. 87
Chapter Ten 95
Chapter Eleven 101
Chapter Twelve.. 107
Chapter Thirteen 117
Chapter Fourteen 125
Chapter Fifteen.. 135
About the Author 140

Oaths

New York Attorney Oath

I do solemnly swear (or affirm) that I will support the constitution of the United States, and the constitution of the State of New York, and that I will faithfully discharge the duties of the office of [attorney and counselor-at-law], according to the best of my ability.

New York Judge Oath

I do solemnly swear (or affirm) that I will support the constitution of the United States, and the constitution of the State of New York, and that I will faithfully discharge the duties of the office of judge, according to the best of my ability.

Federal Attorney Oath

I, AB, do solemnly swear (or affirm) that I will support and defend the Constitution of the United States against all enemies, foreign and domestic; that I will bear true faith and allegiance to the same; that I take this obligation freely, without any mental reservation or purpose of evasion; and that I will well and faithfully discharge the duties of the office on which I am about to enter. So help me God.

Rules of Professional Responsibility

New York Rules of Professional Responsibility

https://www.nysba.org/DownloadAsset.aspx?id=50671

Model Rules of Professional Responsibility

https://www.americanbar.org/groups/professional_responsibility/publications/model_rules_of_professional_conduct/model_rules_of_professional_conduct_table_of_contents/

Chapter One

The first thing we must do is kill all the lawyers. – Henry VIII, William Shakespeare

Send lawyers, guns and money. – Warren Zevon

Let me get right to the point as it concerns New York litigators. Litigators are the outside the office lawyers who most of the time are appearing before judges and doing depositions. This is opposed to your inside lawyers who stay in the office drafting documents.

A New York litigator is like the Right Stuff test pilot of the legal profession. We walk through the halls of the court house with a swagger before the court rooms open where all the litigators are lined up in the halls in front of their assigned court eyeing each other, nodding, making note of a super star and making chit chat with a colleague all dressed immaculately and in deep concentration reviewing their action plan for the morning.

As you pass colleagues you say hello. Today they are your friend tomorrow they are your opponent it is the way of the legal profession. You are a hired gun representing a good guy one day and a bad guy the next and the same holds true for your colleagues. Spin the wheel on any given day and everyone's roles change.

The regular litigators are a fairly small group. Probably numbering in the hundreds city wide. You can see this being the number by going to the general calendar call in the main court room when a few hundred cases are called and each attorney has one or two cases at most.

So yes, you are a litigator and a lone wolf of sorts. But the pack comes together if threatened from the outside and yes we do eat our own dead. So don't mess with a litigator. And in the words of Justice Charles Kuffner, Never bullshit the bullshiters.

Now being a litigator anywhere is like playing in the major leagues but litigating in New York is like playing ball in the American League East. You know the teams here, the Yankees, the Red Sox, the Orioles. So you are the top of the food chain like a member of Seal Team Six.

I might seem a little cocky but that is the mindset of a successful litigator. You are an alpha personality, there are no crunchy betas here, for long at least. Let's face it, do you want a rabbit as your attorney or a man eating tiger. You decide, it's your case, it's your money, it's your liberty.

You may think I am cocky but most litigators are the same way. Case in point, I am a Brooklyn guy and I go to Queens Supreme for a case. One of the top litigators there comes up to me and shakes my hand and we start making small talk but at one point he says this is all mine from there to there to there to there pointing to each side of the court house. You see he's a Queens guy and I am a Brooklyn guy and this is Queens not Brooklyn.

Being cocky does not mean you get into theatrics in front of the judge. This isn't some California court where one hotdog attorney turns a case into a media circus acting like Cicero. No, this is New York and if you start getting theatrical the judge will rip your head off and throw it threw a window. Rule one for New York is to practice with an even tempered keel.

That doesn't mean we are weak we are strong but calm and deliberative in front of a judge but this rule can get thrown out on occasion as we will see a little later. When I was a judge we had a young New Jersey attorney not admitted to practice in New York want to come in and present a case. Well, I decided to test her timber and pushed back against her request but she pushed back and then I pushed back but she came right back and was determined to do a case in New York. In the end I determined she had the right stuff and granted her request. She went on to win her case.

My deference to judges goes back to my Moot Court training at Brooklyn Law School where through deference you were better able to convince a judge rather than by arguing with them. You know, you catch more flies with honey.

You could see this in the Ruth Bader Ginsberg movie On the Basis of Sex. And that is how I even got on the Moot Court team was by showing deference to the judges and winning and saving the life of a minor who was mentally challenged who Texas wanted to make healthy so they could execute him.

And yes, everyone hates attorneys except for their own attorney who's going to pull them out of the gutter and carry them to dry land. We are probably the most hated profession but when you are in a jam only a lawyer is going to get you into a better place. Believe me you want us in the trenches with you, we got your back my friend. You may not have us into your house for dinner but you'll give us that house to stay out of jail. Right.

This brings to mind the Who song, Behind Blue Eyes about being the bad guy. When I retired as a judge and lawyer I did some teaching and boy what a different world that is everyone loves you and holds you up on a pedestal.

But again, a teacher is not who you turn to when you're in a legal entanglement. They have their purpose and we have ours sort of like the CSNY song about the eagle flying with the dove. An eagle will dive down from a mile up in the sky and crash almost into the water to catch a fish while the doves sit on the ground pecking at seed mixed in with dirt. Who do you choose to go into the trial arena with an eagle or a sparrow, you decide?

Chapter Two

Ok, enough with the Right Stuff talk let's get down to the brass tacks of litigation. Let's talk about litigator lingo. When I was an intern in law school an attorney asked me to do a motion in limini. No one could tell me what a motion in limini was. There was nothing in the case law, form books or even the law dictionary. It ended up that I didn't carry out that assignment.

But I never gave up on the search for the answer. It came quite accidently to me while I was studying some Roman texts thirty years later. In Limini means in Latin at the start of. So it was a preliminary motion but it was no longer in common usage so that is why no one knew what the hell it was but I now knew and I guarantee you the lawyer who gave me the assignment had no clue what it was other that a dead end assignment. Sort of like we in the Boy Scouts used to call a snipe hunt.

Now more lingo is the names of the courts. Kings County State Supreme is called Kings Supreme. And Supreme Court in Queens is Queens Supreme. In Brooklyn the criminal court is called Brooklyn criminal and civil is Brooklyn civil. Landlord Tenant court is L & T. The Federal District Court in Brooklyn is called the Eastern District and in Manhattan it is called the Southern

District. The Second Department Appellate Court is called Monroe Place after the street it is on. In Supreme Court each court room has a number so if someone says what court you're going to you rarely say the judge's name but say Part 30 or Part 35. And Supreme Court judges are not judges but justices. Administrative Law Judges are called ALJs but are really defined by civil service as hearing officers. A JHO is a judicial hearing officer sort of an ALJ in State Supreme, but there is also the special referee who is also a quasi-judicial officer. The law secretary for the justice is really the law clerk. A Court Street attorney is meant as a term to mean a shyster. But in reality your Court Street attorneys are some of the best litigators in the city whose main goal is never to leave any problem unsolved. In Supreme the Chief Administrative Judge is not an ALJ but the chief judge, unless you're talking about the Chief Judge of the Court of Appeals. In administrative court the chief ALJ is really called the chief judge. An arbitrator or mediator is not engaged in arbitration or mediation but Alternative Dispute Resolution. But what's a federal magistrate? I don't know, who's on first.

In case you're wondering why the LSAT exam asks questions about a man in a red hat sitting next to a woman in a blue shirt across from a man in a yellow shirt sitting next to a woman in a purple hat.

Well, the previous paragraph should give you an idea why. Lawyer logic. You get the picture, let's move on. And of course I have been told that many of these titles have now changed since I practiced.

Chapter Three

So as a litigator your day is spent outside the office but you do check into that office in the afternoon to do follow up and look over the next day's court appearances. Really top litigators work after hours doing small claims cases in so called night court which is really civil court. There is nothing like having an opponent who wants his day in court in front of a judge and is willing to keep you up in Bronx civil until 2AM.

These litigants can settle and walk away with something but choose to roll the dice and often lose and walk away angry. Riding the subway home at 2AM from small claims court is something right out of the movie Warriors especially if you are heading home to Brooklyn from the Bronx.

I worked hard litigating in state supreme, civil, family court, small claims and on top of that networking around the clock so that I became a judge in 2000 at the New York State Division of Human Rights. My big achievement here was to close out a ten year old thousand page case that had been passed over by ten judges because it involved a police officer in a reverse discrimination context. The officer claimed his female supervisor was sexually harassing him and denying him a promotion. He had a picture of her looking at him dance at a party. Someone did this to me in college as a joke so I knew it was easy enough to create a picture like this.

But what I really found was that he never told anyone about this not even his long time police partner and most importantly his long term work performance was poor. The supervisor had nothing to do with his being passed over for a promotion it was his performance record. I ruled against him.

My other achievement was pushing settlement to the point I had a huge case load because most everything was settling. I would tell the litigants you can go to trial and one will win and one will lose in a roll of the dice or you can settle and have a win win for the parties. I understand that settlement is now policy at Human Rights.

At the State Employment Relations Board my big accomplishments were unionizing 100,000 child care workers and saving live music in New York City. It was never said but people were wondering why I treated the bargaining unit the way I did in child care workers case. It was because based on the database I saw that it was a transient group of people within the unit. One address when the card was signed but another when the database was submitted but the same person nonetheless. As the fact finder I was within my rights to make such a decision.

On a more sour note, I am told by the conductor of the Hudson Valley Philharmonic that there is no more live music on Broadway. Well I did my best and kept it live while I held the post.

My next assignment was at Unemployment at the height of the Great Recession crisis. The dike had blown open on this and a lot of desperate people were coming into the system we did a great job helping those in need at this time within the parameters of the law. I got this job by telling the chief judge that I never lost a case as an attorney and was never reversed on appeal as a judge. He just looked at me and said you just haven't stretched. I wanted to tell him how much I stretched with the child care worker case but didn't. Nevertheless, I did get that job.

While in law school I interned for a judge in Staten Island, Charles Kuffner. I hit it off with his clerk Richard Fuchs who wrote a seminal book on the Civil War Confederate commander Bedford Forest accused of atrocities. We spent hour talking law and history. My assignment here was a Speedy Trial motion. No matter how I counted the days the ADA had blown the statute and taken too long to address the case and it was dismissed. Judge Kuffner was a minor league baseball fanatic and predicted teams would come to New York. Sure enough they did, the Staten Island Yankees and the Brooklyn Cyclones. He got me hooked on minor league baseball and today I have season tickets to the Hudson Valley Renegades each season.

In the middle of my judgeships I took off time to work for Justice Robert Kreindler at Kings Supreme. He was on the bench for over thirty years and before that he was a federal prosecutor. He was a tough judge but an animal lover with a heart of gold. He loved going to Broadway musicals. He and I both had weekend homes in the Catskills and would spend time talking about those enchanted mountains. He did say that if the secretary made a typo I would be fired and if he got reversed because of my work the same thing would happen to me. Needless to say I served with distinction until the end of his term upon reaching his mandatory retirement age. Oh the fun thing here was that his secretary was my old secretary at the first law firm I worked for Erica Goulding. She was a jazz fanatic and had a friend with a jazz record store in Toronto and he would ship down dozens of straight up jazz CDs for her each month.

I bring up all this judicial stuff because at orientation for Brooklyn Law School they told us that the school was known for producing judges. I laughed at this and never considered that I would one day be a judge but sure enough I became one. And much of my ability comes from my Moot Court training at Brooklyn Law School. My teams performed well beyond expectations.

The big thing that happened at Judge Kreindler's chambers was when the court officers called to say that a man who the judge had sentenced many years ago wanted to see him and thank him for changing his life. The judge calmly told them to send him up. He told us what was happening and had me sit between him and where the felon was going to sit while the judge leaned back in his chair with his feet up over a drawer where he had a loaded pistol. It would be difficult for the felon to get through security with a weapon but we weren't taking chances. My job was to pounce if the felon made a move while the judge reached for his hardware. The guy came in and was talking nonsense while holding a bag under his arm the whole time. Well he left without incident but we found out that the day he visited us he shot two of his neighbors over loud music. Court Street could really be a Wild West Town at times.

People think lawyering was an easy profession but it could be dangerous. We had one case at Kuffner's part where the defendant was found guilty and he grabbed his lawyer by the neck and started banging his head on the table they were seated out. I talked to one defender and he said he would like to cut half these defendant's fingers off but he still did his job defending them to the best of his abilities.

Every Thursday every legal professional on Court Street including most of Brooklyn Law School were at O'Keefe's

Bar letting off steam. There were ADAs rubbing elbows with public defenders and personal injury lawyers side by side with insurance defense lawyers and you get the drift.

I ended up leaving the judicial field after about ten years and took a job working as the supervising attorney for special investigations back at Human Rights. We took ten year cases and closed them out or sent them down for trial. Thirty percent of our cases went to trial which was way over the norm of 2 percent.

After my job ended, the President Obama funding had ended, I went into teaching and taught at Fordham live and with China and Taiwan by a special Skype type program. Today I am retired and cannot practice law but I do steer people in the right direction and help people as much as I can.

And I am suing the promoters of the Rolling Stones concerts at Met Life Stadium at Human Rights on the charge of disability discrimination. There were not enough disabled seats and the few there were cost five times more than a regular ticket price. I ended up on the cover of the Daily News. And I can just say this much, the Ruth Bader Ginsberg film inspired our legal strategy for that case and of course Keith Richards book where he tells the world of he and the Stones legal strategies over the years.

Like General Patton said to Rommel
upon defeating him in a tank battle, I
read your goddamn book Rommel, I can
likewise say to Keith Richards I read
your goddamn book.

Chapter Four

Let's talk about my legal history. My first trial was in a small civil court on Staten Island. I took the ferry across the harbor passed Ellis Island and the Statue of Liberty and watched as a huge cruise ship went by with like a thousand people dancing to music on its top deck. Me? I was going to work.

The case was about an insurance company that did not want to pay my client for his house that had burned down. The company complained that it was the homeowner's daughter who caused the fire because she had lit a candle.

My opponent who represented the insurer arrived but he was in bad shape. It was as if his entire suit was being unwound by a single thread which trailed after him for ten blocks. It would only be a matter of time before his entire suit would have disappeared.

I presented my case and won it. The insurance company appealed to the appellate term. I prepared my case for appeal as I had been taught in Moot Court Honor Society. We both went in and agreed with the judge to argue on the written briefs. Again I won and the case was reported in the New York Law

Journal. My moment in the sun had arrived.

I practiced in almost every court in all five boroughs of New York and occasionally got to take a drive out to the scenic suburbs for a court appearance or conference. In the city I was in supreme, civil, criminal, family, landlord tenant, small claims and administrative courts.

The toughest courts to be in were the family courts where nobody was happy and the kids were all crying and the parents distraught. I had one couple that just fought each other for the sake of fighting without a care for what was going through the minds of the kids.

Criminal court was mostly DWIs for my clients. When they first turned the lights on in this court you would see a million or more roaches scattering away from the light. Usually I knew the ADA on duty from law school and two things would happen. First they would agree to dismiss the case outright or secondly, the judge would dismiss it after six months of good conduct. Most clients were happy with those outcomes. I did have one client who did not like her resolution and she was yelling at me and it was very embarrassing. The Court Officers escorted her out of the court house. She did not pay us but we had gotten most of our fee upfront.

I have always had a code as a litigator and that was to practice to the best of my abilities. You had to remember you were a hired gun and did not always have a good guy for a client. You could see this really clear at election time with the election lawyers who were mostly all Democrats but who worked for whoever was paying out.

My firm was very political the head partner's father was a congressman from the area who got beat by Hugh Carey who would go on to become governor. He would also give birth to the rise of Mario Cuomo who was his Lt. Governor. Cuomo's main benefactor was his law partner who you would see walking Court Street regularly. The big names among New York election lawyers were Marty Connors, Aaron Maslow, Bob Muir and a few others I cannot recall. You were not always one of the Magnificent Seven, sometimes you were the police chief from Casablanca. C'est la vie.

So of course defense lawyers are not pro criminal. They are just doing their job. As I said earlier one lawyer said he would like to cut off his client's fingers. He defended that guy to the point that the judge let the guy go.

You fought to the best of your abilities like an ancient Greek mercenary. Your culture and kleos or honor are more important than being on the right or wrong side. You will recall that many Greeks fought for the Persians who fought the Athenians, the Spartans and in the end Alexander the Great.

What is kleos. It is Greek word for a special kind of glory. It is best seen in the Iliad by Homer where Athena tells Achilles she has seen his future and he has two choices. One is to fight like a great warrior but live a short life while being famous. The other was to just go home to his goat herds and forgo fighting the Trojans and with that he would live a long life as an unknown person. I think you can see which way your New York litigator would go.

We talked earlier about the felon who visited Justice Kreindler and our fear he might be armed. Well at that point in court history security was as strict as an airport. But it wasn't always that way. When I was first starting out there was no security but then they put in the barriers and not everyone knew that they were up so you would be on line waiting to go through when someone would get off the line and go into a nearby bathroom and you would hear the sound of a heavy metal object hitting the bottom of the trash can in there.

My wife Jeri tells a story of Grand Jury duty when one suspect went crazy and the ADAs had trouble controlling him and they had to hold the doors shut to keep him out. They were barely able to hold him before court officers arrived. Never a dull moment.

Chapter Five

Now Landlord Tenant court or L & T court if you will is an important arena for any general practice attorney. Yes there are firms that specialize in this area and between you and me they do pretty good and really know their stuff.

For instance, one time over in L & T an attorney who specialized got my case dismissed because of a minor typo. I didn't lose the case but had to start the entire proceeding over again starting with a new petition.

Now my greatest L & T case was for a group of Jamaican tenants who had a really bad landlord who really let everything run down. No hot water, heat, vermin and peeling paint. These clients were desperate. They were a step away from homelessness. I came in and fought it out for months with the entire time the clients not having to pay rent.

In the end the judge ordered that the tenants live in the apartments rent free for six month until they could find new comparable housing and then the landlord would pay for their move. Talk about a stick in the eye of a bad guy. Man I was a hero to these tenants to the degree they wanted to march me through Brooklyn at the head of the Caribbean Day parade. Well, I exaggerate a little. But they really thought a guardian angel had visited them.

But really it is what the landlord wanted. He wanted them out so he could convert to luxury co-ops. So in the end he got what he wanted and the clients were treated in a humane civilized fashion.

In fact, many of the L & T judges are very big hearted, while still staying within the law of course. New York City housing court is so much different than other jurisdictions where you're pretty much thrown into the street in the middle of a blizzard.

So being a good litigator means thinking outside the box. But this does not apply just to the law part of being a lawyer but the business and marketing end as well. Yes lawyers are also businessmen and good ones at that.

The most important thing to do as a young lawyer is to bring in the business. Once you have established your reputation business will come in on its own but until than you have to promote and market yourself. Don't forget what P.T. Barnum said, you can have the greatest thing in the world but it will be meaningless unless you promote it.

Running an ad in the local paper or the church bulletin will help but you really have to think outside the box and go beyond that. When I first started out it was just before email took off, faxing was still the big thing.

So I created a one page newsletter called the Court Street Sheet which I faxed out to about fifty lawyers. The newsletter would give advice and make suggestions and tell a little news. It was a big hit with the old timers who thought the fax machine was magic, forget what they thought about email a few years later or what we have today.

So a lot of business started coming in. One of my biggest benefactors was Frank Giordano who was a big wheel in the American Legion. I walked in to his office and he knew every detail of my dad's World War II military service even though his records were destroyed with many other GIs in the big records fire many years ago.

Frank would have me handle cases for him and he would hook me up with his buddies. He always wanted me to get tougher with the judges be a little more combative. That might have been good for him but I couldn't pull that off. He fought one judge so severely that he was thrown out of the court room even as the judge called him a lion of the legal profession. I do that and I lose my license.

Frank would also sit me down and have me draft documents which were my weak point but he was able to improve my skills using his old school drafting techniques. Like he would throw a scenario at me and I would draft my way through it.

Frank was also famous for being the lawyer who kept gays from marching in the St. Patrick's Day parade in New York.

His case was in the casebooks with his name. He was very proud of this. I dare tell him that I was one of the leading gay rights advocates in Brooklyn. Best to let sleeping dogs lie.

I don't think it would have mattered to him he was a senior enough lawyer to know the hired gun rule and that one day he might be on the other side of the issue like so many people were in the end when we legalized marriage equality in New York State.

One time in civil court I tried to act a little more Giordano with the judge and had mixed results. I kept talking to her with my finger pointing upwards and

she kept yelling stop pointing at me and
I would say I am not pointing at you
with my finger pointing upward. She
became furious and sent us down to her
clerk for conference.

We came back from conference and I
had a favorable disposition but she was
still mad and yelling about my finger
which was still pointing upward. For ten
minutes we went back and forth: stop
pointing at me, I am not pointing at you,
stop pointing at me, I am not pointing at
you on and on until she said get the hell
out of this courtroom and off I went but
I did have my favorable settlement
agreement.

I got tough with a judge another time and we did get a favorable response from the client who was hundred percent in the right to the point there was no way the judge was going to bend anything the other way. The client threw me a pair of tickets, front row center to Ragtime on Broadway. The tickets were worth more than my fee so maybe there was something to Frank's insistence on being tough with judges.

Chapter Six

The best legal office addresses on Court Street were 16, 32 and 26 with 16 being the top of the food chain. Again, my first job was at 32 Court Street with Dorn and Associates. My boss was Steve Dorn whose father was the last Republican congressman from this area. He was swept into office with Eisenhower and defeated years later by Hugh Carey who had a date with destiny as governor of New York and the buy who tapped Mario Cuomo to be is Lt. Governor. Cuomo's king maker was located at 16 Court which is where Governor Cuomo once practiced law. Yes, some powerful people were Court Street attorneys.

Dorn shared his office with the Republican chairman of Brooklyn Arthur Bramwell. Arthur was the last of the gentleman politicians. His brother Hank was a federal judge. Arthur and I became good friends and he asked me to form a club in Brooklyn Heights with another Republican Mark Uncapher who was also an attorney out of Buffalo. They also tapped me to run for the assembly which is how I made a name for myself. I was an activist for the Young Republicans and with their help we did better than any other Republican running in that district where Democrats led by 3 to 1.

I campaigned with another attorney Barbara Grceivic who was running for judge. She did well but fell short also. She was the person who got me the job with Justice Kreindler. She was his law clerk but got a position with another judge. She was a world traveler and used to run foot races all over the globe from Antarctica to Easter Island. She had a powerful legal mind and would have made a great judge.

Dorn used to like the fact that I wore a Yankees cap and hired me to work in his office. He trained me along with his drafting guy a JHO named JB. I learned the fundamentals of the law practice. This was good because I had been looking for job since before I was admitted to the bar. I wasn't making a lot of money but I was learning and that was more important.

To make a long story short I ended up going out on my own taking over the office of my friend Jeff Stichinsky who became a special referee. You could fit into that office with a shoe horn but the rent was low and it was a 26 Court Street address. Jeff and I would eat out once a month for dinner at the Second Avenue Deli and then go up to Brooks Brothers where he would buy a suit or some shirts and I would buy a tie. Brooks Brothers was the place to be seen. A who's who of city attorneys. Jeff wanted to be a judge also like

Barbara. They didn't want to be any old kind of judge but State Supreme.

Eventually I moved into a suite of attorneys headed by Mark Stofsky who I knew from 32 Court who were located at 175 Remsen just off Court. This was a large office but I was earning only enough to pay my rent. So when Arthur offered me a judgeship at Human Rights I jumped on it thinking it would be a noble calling and a decent pay check. Which it was on both accounts.

So I landed the job in state service as a human rights judge. The other attorneys in my suite were mad that I was leaving because it meant a vacant office. But Jeff came in and smoothed things over and they saw that I was not doing well in private practice and that I had to into state service. Besides in a few weeks they found an attorney to take my place.

You had all kinds of characters on Court Street. One was this guy Harry. He was an elderly British man with a huge beard. He sold magazine subscriptions to all the lawyers for their waiting areas. Everyone loved it when he rolled into your office with his lists of hundreds of magazines. It was like when you were a kid and the Scholastic Book people came to your classroom with all their book titles. I would always order a subscription or two from him since I was in magazine publishing before I went to law school.

Another institution on Court Street was the Brooklyn Bar Association. They were a wonderful group of people and the membership was quite reasonable. If you didn't have a law office you could use one of their conference rooms to meet clients. You could use one of their larger rooms to host big events. They put on great CLE courses and gave you the opportunity to put together one on your own.

Though I am in retirement I still keep a foot in with these legal associations belonging to the Dutchess County

Magistrates Association which is dedicated to all types of judges in my county. As of this writing I am trying to rejoin the Brooklyn Bar Association just because they were an excellent group and for purposes of nostalgia. I would like to join the New York State Bar Association but their prices are too high for someone on a fixed income. I may try and negotiate a special rate with them. The state bar put out great lawyer's practice manuals sort of like the bar exam manuals you got in bar review which covered every area of law. They had general practice ones and focused ones like real estate or personal injury.

One event everyone looked forward to was the annual gala at Brooklyn Borough Hall. This was a great event to meet many of the judges in the county from supreme to civil to criminal. This was a beautiful building with a great interior making it feel like you were at the United States Supreme Court in Washington.

In the middle of all of this was Brooklyn Law School. You know I saw the Ruth Bader Ginsberg movie and they were making a big deal today that 40 percent of the new Harvard law school class there were women. Thirty years earlier at my school we had a 50:50 ration of men and women. In fact the top people at the Moot Court Honor Society were women and we had a really winning reputation across a wide array of completions.

My team was the corporate securities team and we made it to the quarter finals at Fordham which was beyond expectations. We had to write a brief and then break up the oral arguments so that each member of the team took part. My team had two guys and one woman. They liked the job we did so much that they made me the coach for the team the following year. Both years the issue was variants on insider trading which was a big topic back in those days.

Moot Court was like the athletics of law school as opposed to the intellectualism of law review and law journal. The key to our success was practice, practice, practice. Write, write, and re-write. Also great interaction with the professors. My team worked with a former SEC Board member Professor Karmel and professor Pinto who was some kind of corporate securities genius. We also had a great appellate advocacy professor Ursula Bentley who was famous for her work against capital punishment. And let's not forget the writing professors who are like the baseball scouts who find the diamonds in the rough who will go on to make Moot Court Honor Society. My instructor was Professor Areola who gave me my highest mark in law school.

Brooklyn Law was famous for hosting the Jerome Prince Evidence competition. All the Moot court teams had to volunteer as support for the competition. One year it was in the middle of a blizzard but every one made it in and the competition went on.

When you got accepted into a law school the first thing you would do would be to watch all the first year law school movies like Paper Chase and One L. Fear was the big theme in these works so that when you were at orientation you were trembling as the dean took to the stage. Our dean was Dean Trager who went on to become a Federal judge. In fact he swore me into the Eastern District a year after I was admitted to the state bar. But anyhow he got up on stage and said like in the movies look to your left look to your right one of you will not be here in a year. Then he roared with laughter and said if that was true none of you would be here. The One Ls roared back in applause. And it was true. Only one person dropped out of my class of 300 people and he dropped out to work in his dad's business, he was actually an A student. Just didn't like studying law.

Then there were the restaurants of Court Street and nearby Montague

Street. These were places of celebration and communal gathering. For months almost every lawyer was captivated by the OJ trial sitting and eating and drinking all day in these restaurants watching the spectacle as their practices rotted away.

Then on the other hand were the celebrations. You won a big trial you take every one to the Queen Restaurant for a magnificent Florentine feast. Everyone went the lawyers, the investigators, the secretaries. And in Brooklyn everyone had to have a side of broccoli rabe. Oh and did the wine flow. Pinot Grigio was in big demand until everything collapsed into a 1920s wormwood shooters festival.

And of course you're not the only firm celebrating there are other firms and each table is buying drinks and broccoli rabe for the next table. People are shouting out cheers. It was great when your ship came into harbor. But like a gambler who always makes sure you know when they win but never when they lose more often than not for most lawyers your ship would come into harbor and sink. Many ships would come in but not even enter the harbor more often than not.

Chapter Seven

Now towards the end of my solo practice the online research began to gain favor with small law firms. They already dominated the large firms. So up and down Court Street everybody was throwing out their huge book shelves. There was no longer a need for books. I grabbed quite a few off the street to bring back to my apartment for our book collection. Keep in mind this was pre Kindle and Nook.

Now in law school online research was the norm. We used to burn through the research and paper would be printed out by the ton from these research terminals. They would teach you how to use the books before switching you entirely over to online research. Sort of like showing you how to use a slide rule before giving you a calculator. The books were like a steam locomotive that went 35 mph and the online systems were 100 mph super trains.

By the end of the 90s online had pretty much completely taken over the legal industry. In state service we still had our book library but everyone was wired into and using online research. The state was really tech savvy constantly updating your computer system and online capabilities. It took me a matter of minutes to check all the cases in the closing briefs of trials I had conducted.

It would have taken days a few years earlier.

Even old school Supreme Court Justices like Kreindler were using the online research to a degree. I would look up to his amazement the case law on an issue that came up in the middle of a trial in just a few minutes. But I couldn't show it to him in a print out or on his computer. I had to pull down the books and look up the cases in the books that I found online. Easy enough and he was the boss.

The clerk's offices were going digital which was really big. Going to the file room in the old days was like going into a monastery to find an ancient Roman text. In other words it was archaic. Calendar calls became easier too and was finding your assigned court room. By 2000 the New York legal world was digitally seamless. We were walking upright.

Chapter Eight

Another way to make some extra money before and after court room time was to do foreclosure sales. These are usually a snap with no bidders and the property just going to the bank. If a bidder does show up it is usually done in cash and you take the money to the bank and open a temporary escrow account until you can get it over to the bank in a closing.

This sounds easy enough but a friend of mine went to the bank and the teller said you have the wrong amount here and he went back to a stand to recount the money when some guy went by and said you dropped some money and my friend saw some cash on the ground and bent over to pick it up while realizing these were one dollar bills and his proceeds were all twenties. When he looked back at the stand his entire proceeds were gone. Security cameras showed that it was a team of criminals that did the hit on him. He was stuck owing the money to the bank. No way out.

The state and city courts are a little more relaxed than the federal courts in their rules and conduct in the court room. If you are late in state court you will just be called again on the second calendar call. But in federal court you are given a dressing down. Don't mess around with those federal judges.

On a per diem case I was once given the wrong information by a paralegal on a bankruptcy case and when I stood up and said my statement to the judge he exploded and ripped me to shreds in front of the entire courtroom.

Involvement in groups or networking is very important for a lawyer. It is not just a 9 to 5 job it is a way of life that goes 24 7. That means you got to get out there and meet people. This can be done through politics and/or the bar associations.

At one time or another I was politically active and member of several state and city bar organizations. You can just go to meetings or take CLE courses or attend parties. A bolt of lightning does not come down from the sky to make you a judge. You have to get out there and be Charley hustle. View it as civic work and that will make it easier.

Now the fact is you don't have be active to become say an ALJ. You just have to sign up for the legal specialties civil service exam. It is just a series of questions that try to pin point you area of expertise. It is not an IQ test. But keep in mind if comes down to two candidates with equal points they will most likely go with the person they may have me or heard about prior to the job posting. Just saying.

Chapter Nine

You can still help people after you retire from practice. For instance, there was a group of independent taxi drivers at the local train station who were being forced out by a big corporate taxi operator who got a permit from the MTA. I didn't give them legal advice but I told the independents that they had to go to a hearing and argue their position. I told them they would need evidence also. And the best evidence would be photographs of all the empty taxi stalls and all the waiting customers. Well they plead their case and they were allowed back in the station and now train riders are happy to because when they get off their train there is a cab waiting for them.

I have another case I am thinking of nudging along. They put in a crosswalk near the station to help a young family get safely across the street to be picked up by the bus. Unfortunately, there is no space between the crosswalk and the parked cars so that anyone crossing just appears out of nowhere. This is definitely a code violation. After all don't you remember the campaign against jay walkers back in the 60s where they would say cross at the corner not in between. Well this is in between, parked cars. I think the cross walk sign is not clearly visible either.

Not everything you do has to be legal oriented. A good lawyer knows how to work the levers of government. In Brooklyn a civic leader passed away and the family and friends asked me get a street sign named after him put up. Well, I had to go to the local councilman, the mayor's office, a city council committee and the mayor's office and finally we had a signing ceremony at city hall authorizing the sign and we all got signing pens from the mayor. Then the mayor's community assistance people came in and did the unveiling of the sign. The whole neighborhood turned out and then we had a party afterwards in local social club.

Well I moved up to the suburbs and the family of the first African American mayor of Fishkill says it would be nice to have a sign named after him.   I said I think I could do that. I send an email to the village clerk asking the process for such a request and in five minutes I get a response that the mayor likes the idea and ask that what name do they want on the sign – street, road, land, place, etc. Well in about a month the sign was up and the entire family and all the local elected officials turned out for the unveiling.

When I first moved up to this historic village I said they should have historic welcome signs as you enter the village like the historic Three Village community on Long Island and Brooklyn Heights has. I presented my pitch to the Fishkill Historical Society and they took it to the village. Well, boom, they just happened to have Greenway money and the signs went up within months. Nice painted historical wood signs.

Last year I started noticing book boxes popping up around the mid-Hudson Valley. They were called Little Free Libraries. You take a book and put a book back in or just take a book or just leave a book. I called the village clerk and emailed her a photo of a few of them and she sent it down to the planning commissioner. It was conditionally approved. It had to be eight feet back from the curb and no signs other than the metal plate that said Little Free Library, Take a Book, Leave a Book.

I went on Facebook and we raised money to buy the box and a post for around $300. Quite a few people donated with one young man, Eugene Marshall contributing quite a large sum. The box and post came and my wife and I dug the hole and sank the post and attached the box. It came with some books and then we added some of our own. At first people thought it was a mailbox but then word got around in about a month books began circulating in and out.

The next thing I did was draft a Universal Declaration of Workers' Rights based on Eleanor Roosevelt's Declaration of Human Rights and the recent Declaration of the Rights of Indigenous Peoples. The local paper printed it and we got a good buzz from that.

Today I am suing on my own behalf the promoters of the Rolling Stones concerts at Met Life Stadium claiming that there were not enough seats for disabled people and that the ones that were available were five times more expensive than regular tickets. I brought the suit to the New York State

Division of Human Rights. It was filed right around Christmas 2018.

I sent out a few press releases and wouldn't you know it the New York Daily News picks up the story under a Michael Gartland byline and it runs on the front page of the paper with my picture and that of Mick Jagger. Well I got my 15 minutes of fame that Andy Warhol used to talk about. And the disabled now will get some redress from these concert promoters.

Chapter Ten

Getting back to those cases where the client throws you a little something extra. I won one case where the client purchased me a Brooks Brothers suit. It fit perfectly and to this day I don't know how he figured out my suit size.

Another thing that was going on with legal technology back in the day was scanning documents. This was making file cabinets obsolete. It was also ending the nightmare of the misplaced document that was never found again. Most of the space of an office back then was occupied by file cabinets so you were freeing up space.

We had a break in at my last office once and they scattered files all over the place. My files were small but I still had trouble getting them all back in order but I noticed a personal letter I had from President Gerry Ford was missing. To this day I don't know if it went into the wrong file or they took it to sell.

The reason I think they took it was because another guy in the suite had all his signed baseballs taken off the wall. Those they recovered from an honest memorabilia dealer. I wrote the Ford Library to see if I could get a copy but they said because it was personal there was no archived copy. That's ok I still have a hand written note from President Jimmy Carter, National Security Advisor Brzezinski and Prince Charles. Now I keep these and other important documents in a lock box.

Another good way to get your name out there is to do articles or letters to the editors or be a regular commenter in a favorite paper. I am Armenian and my comments get some harsh comments from Turks but I always write back that thank god we live in a place where we can express our views. Let's get together for some coffee. Rolling Stones fans were angry but at least their comments were funny with all the coverage I got from the Daily News story.

But the worst remarks I got that were pure hate were the Hillary haters responding to my comments in support of Hillary Clinton. I was one of her organizers in the mid-Hudson Valley and spent four years campaigning for her last run for the presidency. We hit a brick wall on that one but nothing hurt more than the hate in those comments.

,

Today social media is very important. Get a law office Facebook page going and a Twitter account and of course LinkedIn and YouTube and post, post, post until you come up strong on the search engines like Google. But enough with this, Let's get back to the arena, the court room.

Chapter Eleven

A fun thing some bar associations do is have trips to Washington to have attorneys sworn into the United States Supreme Court. Which reminds me. A year after you are admitted to the New York State Bar you can apply to be admitted to the U.S. District Court in your area. For me that was the Eastern District and I was sworn in by former Brooklyn Law School Dean Trager who was now a district court judge. After you are sworn in at the Eastern District you take a subway to Foley Square in Manhattan and get admitted to the Southern District. You can do it in reverse too if you chose.

In New Jersey you get admitted to the state and federal bar concurrently.

To get into a New York Federal Court you need a supporter who will attest to your good character. For me it was the inside lawyer at my first law firm JB the JHO. It was great visiting him at Foley Square. You felt like a real VIP going through his private court room door. But then again when I was clerking for Justice Kreindler it was pretty much a VIP feeling as well coming in the back door of the court room or getting off the elevator at chambers.

A litigator is also a consumer affairs advocate sort of like a supplement to the Consumer Affairs Department or Better Business Bureau.

Most of your car safety and fuel regulations were the result of litigation. This goes for environmental concerns too like I helped Clearwater with some legal work in shutting down the Indian Point Nuclear Reactor. We worked with Riverkeeper on that project.

Lawyers keep bad doctors out of the medical field. My friends the Bonina family are major Med Mal attorneys.

My friend became disabled using a TV exercise device and had to drop out of law school and give up a law career because of the chronic pain of his injury. He took it to court and won a settlement and he also was awarded disability using an attorney who specialized in that filed.

Now one thing lawyers like to do is argue legal issues. One issue I argued recently with retired Justice Alice Fisher Rubin was the legality of conducting a Skype wedding involving the jurisdictions of two different states. The ordained minister was in one state and the couple were in another and it was done via Skype. I felt you could do it under the Freedom of Religion protections of the United States Constitution. Justice Rubin strongly disagreed. I deferred to her on the argument in the end.

Maybe one of you law students out there would like to take this issue on or perhaps a Moot Court professor could make it into a competition.

One odd story, I apply one day for a civil court judgeship and go to the local UPS store and have them photocopy my twenty page application and notarize it and ship it right to the New York Civil Court judge handling the hiring. A couple days later I get a call from the civil court with someone screaming at me was I threatening the judge, did I want to end up in jail. What had happened is my shipment some how got mixed up with a wheelchair shipment and the judge got a wheelchair with my return address and they thought I was making some kind of threat. We agreed to push UPS under the bus on that one once we got it all straightened out. Needless to say I did not get the job. Never a dull moment.

Chapter Twelve

Let's go back in time again to law school. Yes, graduating and passing the bar are the most important thing because your entire future depends on a positive outcome for both of these factors. And don't get me wrong bar review and the exam is very difficult it is like running in a marathon. It can cause real mental strain to the degree that I have been told that they have made the New York bar exam easier or better yet more humane in its vigor.

But the real freak out moment in law school is First Year, One L. This is when they break down your brain and rebuild it into a lawyer's brain. You are taught to think like a lawyer. It is essential that this legal process has a successful outcome or else you're not going to get through the rest of law school or the bar exam or the practice of law. And I am not making this up. Intellectuals have told me that it is true lawyers have a different way of thinking. Perhaps it has something to do with our instruction in the Socratic Method. This is where you answer the question yourself, there is no lecturing.

Once you get through this transformation you find that in your second year you have a lot more reading and that is because you can now handle it because your brain has been retooled. As for the Third year, well it is pretty easy just taking courses that you have not taken yet that are on the bar exam. And that is the difference say between a Brooklyn Law School and Harvard Law School. At Brooklyn the focus is on having you pass the bar exam. At Harvard it is about learning theory and passing the bar is an afterthought. For most of us no bar exam pass, no bucks and no Buck Rogers as they said in the Right Stuff movie similarly. Brooklyn has say a 70 percent pass percentage as opposed to say 50 percent for Harvard.

People asked me after I took the bar exam how I did and I could only say the ball was headed to the foul pole.

Meaning its outcome could go either way, pass or fail. I passed New York and New Jersey. Whew.

At Brooklyn the entire class of around 350 people is broken up into groups of around 30 people each. Somehow the people in charge of this seem to get people of similar interests all together in one group. The big thing in first year is forming a study group of say two or three people. Because my group was all friends our group grew to the full 30. We could not move an inch through the syllabus because there were just too many questions. This caused an explosion among us all and everyone broke up into groups of two or three. The good news we were still all friends and I cherish Thursday nights when our group would go out to party at the local bar O'Keefes or into South Street Seaport's Jeramy's.

Another big thing about law school were internships. I interned at the Richmond County District Attorney's Office, for Justice Kuffner and at the New York Stock Exchange Enforcement Bureau. These were all essential to my training as a practicing attorney. I also had a legal job with an L & T firm in Manhattan generally just answering their huge calendar call. That one year that I had this job, the stock exchange internship, moot court competition and I was taking all my classes at night so I was up late I was burning the candle at both ends and was very tired. This was to the point that during one Stock Exchange trial I started to nod out in the back row. Well people noticed and it went around that I fell asleep during a trial. No one asked me to explain why this happened as just told you. They just tagged me. Years later when I interviewed at Chase the question was implied to me. Oh well.

Just a word about the DA internship. Most of the students were from Brooklyn or St. Johns. Now Brooklyn had a liberal reputation yet most of the interns were Republican and St. Johns has a Republican reputation yet most of the interns were Democrats. Every morning we would argue politics for the sake of good debate not bad intent. The best debater was this Democrat Michael Cussick. Well he went onto become an elected official in Staten Island. His father was also a well-regarded judge on Staten Island also.

Justice Kuffner got me into minor league baseball which he swore was coming to the city. We all thought he was crazy but sure enough both the Yankees and the Mets opened franchises in Staten Island and Brooklyn respectively. Unfortunately for the judge, he retired and moved to Oregon just before the teams opening seasons.

Judge Kuffner's law clerk was Richard Fuchs who was a history buff like me and we used to spend hours talking history. He had written a book on the notorious southern commander Bedford Forest. He gave me a signed copy of the book which I have to this day.

My big project here was a speedy trial motion which no matter how I counted the days showed that the DA had blown the statute and the alleged criminal had to be let go.

Getting back to the stock exchange I worked for a former Bronx DA Sue Light who really taught me about securities enforcement and evidence gathering using Lotus software. Churning was the big thing at that time. The really fun part about this internship other than the fact you were in the famed World Trade Center was that a few floors down from us was the Dean Witter subsidized cafeteria where you could get a full Thanksgiving size turkey meal with all the trimmings for $6. Let's just say I put on a few pounds that semester

Chapter Thirteen

I mentioned how I went from thinking I was going to be a corporate lawyer to actually becoming a general practice attorney doing mostly personal injury cases. Well this is ok. You cannot fight the legal stream you must like a Taoist go with the flow or else you will be broken. So my path led to general practice but I was nonetheless a litigator. And this started in law school where my one job was with and L & T firm. It kind of set the stage.

I remember I thought it was so crude being mixed in with a sea of humanity. But you know this was real legal practice. This was the kind of lawyering done in Dickens' books or that Abe Lincoln did. No $600 haircuts and polished nails here. It was all meat and potatoes. And looking back I wouldn't change a thing except earning a few more dollars than I was back then.

And you know small claims court at night was all right. It was really all your A team litigators who were all in good humor. I mean real life was so much more interesting than staying home and watching Seinfeld reruns. I remember one case where my client lost his carry on bag worth a total of fifty dollars but we got a pair of roundtrip airline tickets to anywhere in the world that airline journeyed to. Needless to say the client treated me to a T bone steak dinner at Embers in Bay Ridge. Yeah. I know it wasn't Peter Lugar's but my wife Jeri had taken me there for my 40th birthday and I could say I have been to the mountaintop.

We had a car and truck dealer for a client were constantly going up to the Bronx for small claims. And every one suing us wanted their day in court. Ah yes you would walk passed a boisterous Yankee stadium and go into night court and come out and everything was closed and desolate and it would be a subway ride right out the movie Warriors from the Bronx back to Brooklyn.

Than the next day you would be in upscale Westchester for a hearing or out to Nassau County for a trial. You might even be doing a closing for the car dealer on Park Avenue worth millions of dollars. But the fun part was like being Atticus Finch and getting down into the weeds or as Pete Seeger used to say the big muddy. You were saving children from abuse, tenants from homelessness, drinkers from jail, injured people from a life of disability and poverty. Or you could be sitting in a cubicle staring at the ceiling.

Did you want to be an Agent of Shield, an Avenger, or a hamster on a wheel going home each night and watching reality TV drinking sugar water and cheese puffs? No you wanted to be Iron Man, a litigator. In the end I reached the top my profession and was a judge and just before I retired I worked for the largest law firm in the world Dentons working on a $2 billion power plant case and raking in the money but I would not trade that for a night with my car dealer buddy in Bronx small claims. There is something about taking a bite of the apple called justice.

And of course you are getting involved politically or with groups like Riverkeeper, Clearwater, the Sierra Club or ADK or with historical preservationists. People want to appoint you to government boards like the Brooklyn Navy Yard or the Environmental Control Board. You really are working with super lawyers at these groups. I met one scientist lawyer who shut down a nuclear plant in New Jersey who was like some kind of Dr. Who figure he was so smart. Definitely a big brain but more than willing to teach the trade.

You know its funny all this nuclear stuff goes back to my college days when I was an organizer for NYPIRG getting people to the big no nukes rally at Battery Park. And Jane Fonda was up on stage saying look here is Pete Seeger and his sloop the Clearwater and thinking to myself what a beautiful ship with that colorful sail and all and forty years later I am doing legal work for them and sailing on the Clearwater and even helping steer it one time. Life is good. So get involved. Get out there and live life.

Chapter Fourteen

There is always the threat of being brought before the disciplinary committee of the bar where you can be suspended or disbarred. One of the big offenses is touching escrow money. There was one attorney whose secretary was taking escrow money but they zapped him nonetheless. Took his license away. Another guy knew he was going to be zapped and resigned from the bar to avoid that outcome. You will also get hung out to dry without blinking an eye for a domestic violence offense. I am so worried about getting zapped, even though I am retired, that I have an unaccounted for escrow of $40 that I will not touch. It will sit there till I die and then go to the state and that's how cautious I am.

There is one newspaper, the New York Law Journal, which is instrumental to your practice. It is sort of like Dr. Who's sonic screwdriver or even his Tardis. Its usefulness is beyond explanation. Another good practice is helping your old law school either by judging Moot Court cases, or working with interns. Pro Bono work is also important. When I had a team of interns working for me at the New York State Division of Human Rights as the supervising investigator for special cases I taught them a thing or two and they in turn taught me a thing or two.

Pro Bono work is important because as LBJ used to say it is a thin line between us and them meaning the homeless. My friend Justice Beth Bonina does great work for Toys for Tots. She was also a super litigator and also the chief judge at the Taxi and Limousine Commission at one time.

Every now and then you would get a celebrity client. For us is was the rock and roller Shadow Morton suing over his song rights. I was the only one in the firm to know who the heck he was and how famous he was. We used to talk all the time and it turned out he was from my hometown, Hicksville on Long Island.

He told me he wrote Leader of the Pack at a railroad crossing waiting for a long train to pass by Grumman Aerospace in Bethpage.

Anyhow we win the case and everyone including Shadow heads out to Hogs and Heifers in Manhattan to celebrate rock and roll style with the super models and the bikers. Everyone that is except me. I got assigned the task of closing the office. And every twenty minutes someone would call in saying what a great time they were having.

The lawyer I worked for liked to take things to the edge including the phone bill paying it at the last minute possible just for the sake of going to the edge. You don't know how many times our phone service went down. I would have to personally go down to the phone company and pay the bill with his law firm checking account.

I asked him why do you do this and he said it was like the movie where the judge takes the helicopter out over the sea and barely makes it back each time. Well that was my boss. Needless to say I had less complex role models like Atticus Finch, Benjamin Cardozo and the lawyer in the original Miracle on 34th Street. Well at least one of them was a real person. I did like the lawyers in Great Expectations and Tale of Two Cities also. And let's not forget Abe

Lincoln riding the circuit out of Springfield Illinois.

If the military is your thing you can join the New York Guard which is a military organization in New York for lawyers mostly. You do legal matters for soldiers. A lot of judges and super litigators were enlisted here. I almost joined but changed my mind at the last minute. I wanted to send a photo of me in uniform home to my mother. Ha Ha.

Many lawyers get excited because they can become a notary without taking the exam. You just have to remember that if you take a bad signature well then you lose your law license unlike a regular notary who just loses their right to notarize things.

Being an adjunct law professor at a college is another way to make money and gain experience. I couldn't break into this field but my friend Justice Bonina did as did an elder lawyer friend down in Bay Ridge. I did get an ESL certificate and was teaching English to via live computer hook up in China and Taiwan. It was 7AM in New York and 7PM in China and that made it perfect for my schedule. Unfortunately the pay was terrible but the experience invaluable and I made some good friends. And it did lead to me teaching ESL at Fordham one summer. This was a real feel good situation because everyone loves teachers as opposed to attorneys.

You can also earn money doing arbitrations and mediations. At one agency I worked out we had one mediation that went on for years. Keep in mind you cannot appeal an arbitrators ruling unless you can show fraud which is nearly impossible. The whole purpose of this alternative dispute resolution is to clear up the court calendars and speed things up and lower legal costs.

There are also per diem judge positions like at the MTA that you can work into your schedule and get some judicial experience on your resume.

Everyone once in a while I would have to go out to the East End of Long Island for a matter and this was very pleasurable. I used get some ice tea and caramel rice puffs and pepperoni for the ride and dream of just hanging up city practice and opening an office in Sag Harbor and living in East Hampton or Greenport. This were very cordial in the Riverhead courts and everyone liked us New York lawyers. They had an aquarium out there to you could visit at lunch time. Nice tea room in Greenport also. Plenty of sunshine, fishing boats and sea gulls.

Chapter Fifteen

The pretrial lawyers strategy meeting was always a lot of fun. Usually a lot of pizza and beer were involved. Most importantly though this is where you laid out your entire action plan from legal theory to jury selection to studying the judge's biography.

And oh yes another good way to promote your law practice was to either be a guest on a public access TV show or have one yourself. I used to go on regularly to my friend Commissioner Beverly Copeland's show. She would control the whole process with one little joy stick, cameras and all while she interviewed me. She liked talking to me about my Catskills book and she always made the point that she did not like being in nature but driving through nature and could I give her some good car driving routes through the Catskill which I always complied with for her and her viewers.

College radio is good and I have been on LIU, Stony Brook and some other school radio shows as well WBAI and WDST. I also did my own broadcast which they would drop into another radio show. I interviewed 250 people on this show.

Occasionally you are honored when some asks you to write a legal recommendation for them to get into law school or land a legal job. This is one of the most serious things you can do but once done you will have a friend and ally for life with that person. It is also a way of putting something back into the system that has taken good care of you.

Nowadays a lot my foreign students from around the world want you to put the recommendation on their LinkedIn page. So that's another reason to be engaged with all forms of social media.

Well I could go on but as you can see being a litigator is more than being a hotshot lawyer practicing law it is a way of life that serves justice to the public.

Q.E.D. Quod erat demonstrandum.

About the Author

Michael Boyajian is a retired attorney and former human rights, labor, and unemployment judge. He has interned for Justice Charles Kuffner and was the law secretary for Justice Robert Kreindler. He has never lost a case, and was never reversed on appeal.

He is the author of 20 books most notably The History of the Armenian Speaking People.

He lives with his wife Jeri Wagner and their three cats in the Hudson Valley where they enjoy their Cicero garden and library.

www.ingramcontent.com/pod-product-compliance
Lightning Source LLC
Chambersburg PA
CBHW030651220526
45463CB00005B/1735